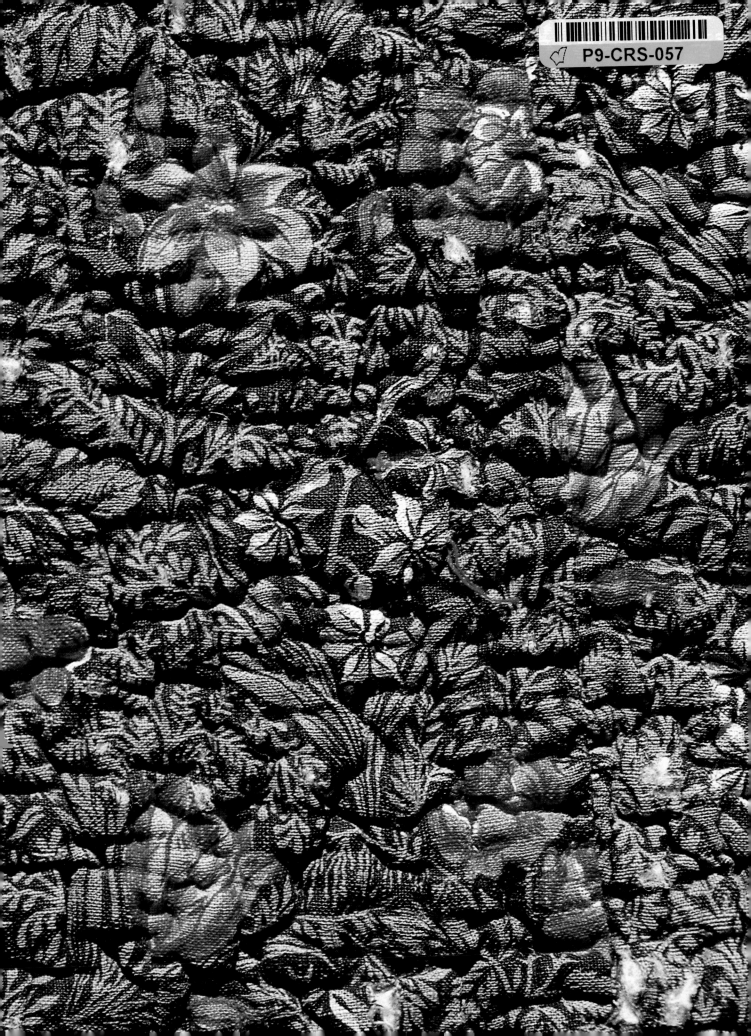

Cooking with Herbs
The Flavor of Provence

for my son Louis Marius Noé

Translated from the French by Josephine Bacon,
American Pie, London
Copy-editing: Christine Schultz-Touge
Color separation: Articolor
Typesetting: Studio X-Act, Paris

Originally published as *Les Bonnes herbes de Provence*
© 2000 Flammarion
English-language edition
© 2001 Flammarion Inc.

ISBN 2-08010-554-X
FA0554-11-01
Dépôt légal: 02/2001

Printed in France by Pollina, 85400 Luçon - n° L82295

Endpapers: Bonnes Herbes,
a cotton fabric, printed in Provence
using wood blocks.
Late eighteenth century.

Michel Biehn

Cooking with Herbs
The Flavor of Provence

Photographs
by Gilles Martin-Raget

Flammarion

contents

The Flavor of Provence

This story begins in the cool air of an early morning in late June. You stride out, leaving the last houses of the village behind you, a knife in your pocket and a canvas or leather *biasse* slung over one shoulder. This knapsack contains a piece of bread, a chunk of goat's cheese, a few tomatoes hastily grabbed from the garden, and a bit of fine salt in a twist of paper—in other words, everything needed for a picnic lunch. You cross a vineyard and skirt the edge of an almond orchard, and then as you hear the sharp rustle of birds disturbed by your step, there you are, at once in the thick of the evergreen oaks, the prickly cedars, and the scrub of the hill country—the *garrigue* of Provence. You find that you are suddenly overcome, something grabs you by the throat, rising straight from the ground through every step you take. It fills your nostrils, then your whole mind and soul, and even moistens your eyes. It is there in the musky fragrance of wild peppermint, the sweet smell of lavender, and the more robust odor of sage. All of a sudden, you crush a clump of pink flowers underfoot,

Basil can be grown in pots from June through late September.

and the subtle odor of thyme rises and blots out all other smells. At each step, the perfumes mingle and combine to further enchant you.

There is hardly a cliché more widely used in today's French cuisine than that of *herbes de Provence*. Souvenir stores and tourist traps abound with uninspiring little sachets, made of printed cretonne for a 'Provençal look' or of burlap for a 'natural look,' and all are labeled 'Herbes de Provence.' The sachets contain an unidentifiable mix of dried herbs, reduced to powder and exuding an indefinable odor, yet supposedly containing all the magical aromas of the wild open countryside of Provence. What a difference you can taste in herbs gathered on the hillsides or grown in gardens—a rich and wonderful natural harvest, and a cultural treasure of Provence—precious gifts of the land and a wonderful reminder of traditional herb lore. The chefs of Marseilles and Avignon know exactly how best to use each herb, alone or in combination with others, to flavor an omelet or a sauce. Grinding herbs to a dust simply to preserve them is the best way of ensuring that they lose all of their aroma. I strongly advise you to preserve fresh herbs whole, in bunches, in airtight metal or wooden boxes, or even in brown paper bags (though never in plastic) away from light and air. The herbs should first be suspended upside down to dry. Such herbs are the wealth, the natural and cultural treasure of Provence, precious gifts of the land and of traditional know-how. Cooking with herbs, combining them, marrying their fragrances and flavors is an art, the result of a long local tradition. Of course it is accessible to any sensitive cook, but, at the very least, it requires a certain initiation period, a touch of knowledge, and some experience.

Herbs have always been picked on the hillsides of Provence and they have long been used to treat the flu, heal a wound, or alleviate pain, as well as to dye fabric red or yellow—to say nothing of flavoring a stew or a pâté. The French title of this book, *Les Bonnes Herbes de Provence*, refers first of all to the fact that most herbs found in Provence are "good herbs." There are very few *mauvaises herbes*—"weeds," or more literally "bad herbs" to be found here. In fact, the people of Provence so loved herbs that in the late eighteenth century, a group of calico fabrics were given the name "Bonnes Herbes." This pattern of tiny flowering herbs was printed using wood blocks on a puce, brown, bronze, or khaki back-ground, and made into quilted comforters, dresses, camisoles, skirts, and voluminous capes that were worn by the beauties of Provence.

This book is first and foremost a cookbook. Although I list the medicinal properties of each herb, tonic or diuretic, stimulant or analgesic, I concentrate mainly on flavor, fragrance, and the thousand-and-one traditional or modern culinary uses. I cook the same way my mother taught me, the way she learned from her own mother. It is a simple cuisine, which celebrates the special and magnificent fragrances of Provence that are so dear to me. To these traditional family treasures, I have added a few excellent recipes for dishes shared in the homes of friends—recipes that make such excellent use of certain herbs that I wanted to share them with you.

But first I shall take you into the hills, high above the plains, planted with grape vines and olive trees, up onto the embankments beside the paths which lead right up to Mont Ventoux and into the heart of the *garrigue*, where each year, on a specific day, we would go and pick our herbs. On Midsummer Day, or the feast day of St. John, we would pick thyme, rosemary, and wild lavender. Michaelmas, the 29th of September, was the day for picking fennel. We knew that on these

The slopes of Mount Ventoux, overlooking the vineyards, are still one of the best places to pick wild herbs (right).

Wild leeks can be gathered beside the little stone outbuildings amid the vines (following double page).

particular days the chosen herb was at its height. All of the personality of Provençal cooking comes from these hillside herbs. They are totally indispensable to it.

Provence has another family of herbs that are less fragrant, slightly bitter, greener, and more tender. These are the herbs of the fields, the little green shoots of spring. Every spring day, local families would go out armed with a large basket and a little knife to collect these herbs. They included lamb's lettuce (mâche) and arugula (rocket salad) for salads, wild asparagus and wild leeks for omelets, young nettles and poppy leaves for gratins, and dandelion flowers for making preserves.

Many of these plants can be found in the gardens of Provence. Herb gardens for the cultivation of "simples" have been tended since the Middle Ages within monastery cloisters or the grounds of French châteaux. Simples were used for the making of liqueurs, elixirs, and herbal remedies. In later years, the local pastor would cultivate camomile, hyssop, and aniseed in the churchyard. Nowadays, thyme and sage, arugula and purslane are grown alongside basil, parsley, coriander, mint, and chives. Since these plants have been domesticated, they have lost some intensity of flavor, although they have sometimes gained in tenderness and

Thyme, savory, and fennel can be picked at the foot of the château of Les Baux.

sweetness. At any event, their cultivation has made them available in the heart of cities and almost year-round.

Thus, most herbs of Provence can now be found freshly picked in market stalls and grocery stores both here in Provence and far away. Although you may not be able to buy wild leeks or young poppy shoots, try out my recipes by using young cultivated leeks or spinach as stand-ins— the result will still be absolutely delicious.

One more word about another plant that is essential for the success of even the most modest of gourmet moments: the grapevine. Although the young spring leaves are delicious when wrapped around all manner of fillings, it is the fruit, and especially the delicious nectar produced from it—wine—that I want to mention here. Today the wines from south-eastern France are rated among the greatest in the country. I have asked my friend, the enthusiastic, passionate, and inspired oenologist, Jacques Machurot, to choose from among the vast array of wines produced in the region (and some from further afield) those that best accompany these flavors from Provence.

HERBS OF THE HILLS
AND HERBS OF THE FIELDS

I am well aware that the ridges of Mont Ventoux, the woods of Sainte-Baume, and the slopes of Garlaban can hardly be compared to the enchanted Brittany forest of Brocéliande, inhabited by Merlin the magician. Yet—having so often found myself lying flat on my stomach on the warm earth, my chin in the dirt and my nose buried in a fragrant clump of thyme, its twisted, woody stem resembling a miniature tree trunk, engrossed for minutes or even hours in witnessing the final metamorphosis of a cicada attached to the foot of a pine-tree—I can assure you that the hills of Provence are a veritable fairyland.

Once upon a time, these hills abounded with stories of miracles and magic spells. There were wise men and women in the villages who knew how to "dispel the fire"— in other words, they could ease the pain of a burn or the fever of sunstroke—or "dispel the blackness," meaning that they could rid a house of bad luck or a curse. There were those who knew how to use plants to alleviate all types of pain and cure all sorts of illnesses. These healers could be found in the early hours of Midsummer Day gathering the herbs, which were then reputed to be at their most potent. Thus, before they were widely used as delicious flavorings for cooking, the fragrant herbs of Provence were the most indisputably effective remedies in folk medicine—so effective that they were sometimes credited with magical powers. For example, in the Middle Ages, a person with a fever was advised to go out for three mornings in a row, at full moon or just before, in search of a clump of mint or oregano. Offerings of bread, salt, and pepper were to be made to the plant, which was then asked to cure the sufferer. After three days, when the clump of oregano or mint had wilted, the fever should have disappeared. This empirical knowledge of the powers of simples eventually developed into more scientific methods.

As late as the nineteenth century, herbalists flourished in all the towns and cities of France, and their raw materials

Wild asparagus.

15

were purchased from the herb-pickers of Provence. The herbalists dried the herbs and stored them in large linen sacks or glass jars. Borage, fennel, juniper, marjoram, mint, oregano, summer and winter savory, sage, wild thyme, and many other local herbs sat alongside the exotic, imported badian, cinnamon, and ginger, making the entire shop smell like an herbal infusion.

Nowadays, most of these shops have disappeared, along with the wise old herbalist in his metal-rimmed eyeglasses surrounded by glass vials, copper scales, and his porcelain pestle and mortar. The art of using simples has been supplanted by considerable developments in chemistry and the influence of pharmaceutical companies. Very few of our old people are still familiar with the secrets of herbs and, in France, only pharmacists are allowed to trade in medicinal plants. Yet curiously, the latest alternative medicines of the new millennium hark back to ancient folk wisdom, thus once again giving these

Wild leek.

Rosemary in flower.

plants the attention and importance they so richly deserve.

Yet at the same time, aromatics and seasonings are ever more in view at the markets of Provence. From spring onward, you will have no problem finding bunches of Provençal herbs tied with string or rafia or planted with their roots in little pots. First and foremost is thyme, the gentle lord of the *garrigue*. This tiny, perennial shrub has a gnarled, woody stem with tiny gray-green leaves, and produces strongly fragrant lilac, pink, or white flowers in high summer—a feast for the bees. Next there is the slender rosemary plant, with its longer, straighter branches, covered in rows of needle-like leaves that are dark green underneath and grayish-green on top; its delicate blue flowers appear in early summer. Then comes sage, with large, rather soft, grayish leaves that feel as though they were cut from a piece of velvet. Summer and winter savory are twins, the former an annual, the latter a perennial; both are used to flavor Banon goat's cheese. There are also oregano and wild marjoram with its rounded, downy leaves that are sometimes tinged with red. Juniper shows up with spherical green berries that turn blue-black in the fall and are used to flavor rabbit terrine and game stews. Fennel grows along the roadside, its tall, elegant stems topped with large yellowish umbelliferous flowers. Finally, there is lavender, better known for its perfume than for its medicinal or gastronomic properties, but whose wonderful bluish-purple color has recently inspired chefs and gourmets to use it in cooking.

There are other herbs in Provence, apart from these fragrant spellbinders of the hills. They are more modest, less flamboyant, greener, and less hardy. They are sometimes mistaken for weeds, yet they do not merely flavor a dish—they can constitute the dish itself. These are the herbs of the fields.

Provence is a dry land in which water is wealth, in which greenery is a rare pleasure, and in which cooking with greens is a celebration and a daily ritual. Green salads are served at every meal and there are innumerable recipes for dishes containing spinach, chard, leeks, and wild herbs. Provençal locals never go for a walk without a sharp paring knife in their pockets. Spring is the best time for picking greens, since the young shoots are at their juiciest. Soil that is regularly tilled, such as vineyards and olive groves, yields wild leeks and purslane. Nettles grow among ruins and in abandoned fields. Dandelions and poppies also appear on plowed ground, in fields, and along the roadside, while wild asparagus hides in the hedgerows and undergrowth.

THYME

Thyme, known as *farigoulo* in Provençal, is used as an olive tree for the Christmas crêche, since it is just the right height to go with the little clay *santon* figures so typical of Christmas in Provence. Its silvery gray-green color, gnarled yet solid trunk-like stem, and its wide, spreading, bushy branches make it an eminently suitable representative of the Provençal landscape in miniature, which the children of Provence create every year at Christmas, using moss and pebbles, with brown paper for the rocks and silver paper for the rivers.

Thyme is king of the hill, emerging everywhere from between the stones, colonizing embankments and fallen rocks, while carpeting the most arid plateaux with its little gray bushes. Thyme should be picked in April as soon as it begins to bloom with tiny pink flowers, because at that moment its active principles are particularly rich. The people of Provence make an herbal tea from it, which if drunk without sugar does wonders for the digestion, circulation, and insomnia.

Thyme is almost as omnipresent as garlic and bay leaf in the local cuisine. Although its own scent is strong, it mixes well with other fragrances. That is why it is included in every *bouquet garni* used to flavor dishes from stews to bouillabaisse, from daube to ratatouille—including rabbit civet and sausage links with lentils. It is just as suitable for meats as for vegetables and works particularly well with tomatoes. Some of thyme's success is no doubt due to the fact that it keeps so well, so that it can be used all year round. Yet in Provence, thyme is never dried and stored, but picked as and when required. One more word about a close relative of garden thyme, known as mother-of-thyme or wild thyme. Wild thyme looks rather different than garden thyme; its stems are more slender and straighter and its dark green leaves are longer. It is a wonderful aromatic, used in the same way as thyme.

Goat's Cheese with Mushrooms and Thyme

~

This is a delicious fall appetizer. The mushrooms in question are the Blood-Red Milk Cap (*Lactarius sanguifluus*) which are found only in southern Europe. Milk Cap (*Lactarius deliciosus*), which is found all over the temperate zone, can be substituted. Both grow under pine trees among the heather of the Roussillon area, near the Spanish border, and they are sold in local markets throughout the region in September and October. Large Portobello (cultivated) cap mushrooms can be substituted.

PREPARATION. Two mushrooms per person will be needed. Only the caps are used, so keep the stems and trimmings for flavoring an omelet. Carefully clean the mushrooms using a small paring knife to remove any twigs, soil, pieces of leaf, and pine needles. Wipe the caps lightly with a paper towel, but be sure not to wash them—

mushrooms should never be washed! Then arrange the caps, gills upward, in a gratin dish. Slice a small, ripe, fresh goat's cheese (Petit Banon is excellent for the purpose) crosswise and place a slice on each mushroom cap. Sprinkle each cheese with a little thyme and that's all there is to it! Cover the dish with a sheet of aluminum foil, making sure that it does not touch the cheese, and bake for 30 minutes in a hot (400°F/200°C) oven.

Serve immediately with crusty, whole-wheat bread and a fragrant white wine, such as a Baux-de-Provence or a Mas-Sainte-Berthe, or the elegant Corbières Blanc of the Château de Lastours which is full and silky in the mouth.

"Wild" Rabbit

~

This is more than a recipe, it's a "trick" for making rabbit bought from the butcher taste wild like hare.

PREPARATION. Stuff the cavity of a whole rabbit with lots of thyme and four or five crushed juniper berries, cover with more thyme, then wrap it in a large sheet of aluminum foil and seal well. Leave the rabbit to rest overnight before cooking in mustard or as a civet.

The wines that best accompany rabbit are a white wine from Provence or Corbières (see above) or even a young red made from Syrah grapes that are fruity yet refreshingly acidulated. It can also be appreciated with the very elegant Costières-de-Nîmes from the Château Mourgues du Grès, which is full-fruited but also has finesse.

Potato *Tian*

~

This very simple dish combines thyme and bay leaf, rosemary and savory, oregano and sage. Choose eight firm, waxy potatoes. Wash and peel, then slice them

into fairly thick rounds; 1/3-inch thick is about right. Arrange in a greased glazed pottery gratin dish (known in Provence as a *tian*), mixing them with seven or eight small white onions that have been peeled and split in half, and a generous handful of all of the above herbs. The herbs should be dried but left in sprigs; the bay leaves and sage leaves should be whole. Use plenty of thyme, a little bay leaf, sage, and savory, and very little oregano and rosemary.

A little practice and experience will show you how to produce the ideal combination of these herbs.

Add a cup of water to the bottom of the dish, a dash of olive oil over the potatoes, and finally, sprinkle with coarse salt. Bake this *tian* for one hour in a hot oven, adding a few tablespoons of warm water every so often; the bottom of the dish should never be allowed to dry out. Serve hot with a large green salad.

Baked Chicken

~

This delicious dish can be cooked directly in the dripping pan or in a roasting pan in a hot (400°F/200°C) oven. Start by preheating the oven at its hottest setting.

While the oven is warming, cut up a large free-range chicken into about ten serving pieces. Naturally, the success of this recipe depends, above all, on the quality of the poultry, so you will need a grain-fed bird raised in the open air.

Pour a generous stream of olive oil into the bottom of the dripping or roasting pan. Add a cup of hot water and two coarsely chopped onions. Wash, wipe, and trim two eggplant and two zucchini and cut them into cubes. Add to the oil along with three large tomatoes sliced crosswise and ten unpeeled garlic cloves. Arrange the chicken pieces over the vegetables, with sprigs of thyme and rosemary, and a few sage leaves in between. Salt, pepper, sprinkle again with olive oil, and place it in the oven for exactly one hour.

You may need to add hot water from time to time, but it should have evaporated completely by the hour's end.

Roast Chicken

~

This must be the easiest way of flavoring poultry. Choose a large free-range chicken. Clean it out and rub it with a little olive oil. Then stuff with a mixture of hillside herbs: sprigs of thyme, rosemary, and savory, sage leaves, as well as two or three unpeeled garlic cloves, which you have lightly crushed with the palm of your hand to release their aroma. Sprinkle the chicken with salt and freshly ground pepper and truss it before roasting in a hot (400°F/200°C) oven. To roast the chicken, place it in the oiled dripping pan (or roasting pan) and dot it with butter. Roast for between 45 minutes and 1 hour, depending on the size. Baste from time to time with a little hot water, then with the cooking juice. Salt and pepper again just before serving.

Godfather Bertrand's Thyme-Flavored Honeycake

~

This recipe was born when not a grain of green aniseed to flavor a honeycake was left in the house. Our Godfather Bertrand, who was in charge of making this indispensable snack for us that day, had the brilliant idea of adding some tiny leaves from a sprig of thyme instead of the customary aniseed to the batter. The marriage of thyme and honey from the *garrigue* was a particularly felicitous one and so delighted us that Godfather Bertrand abandoned the use of green aniseed in his recipe forever. He continues to bake honeycake and his variation appears not to have upset the ghosts of our grandmothers.

PREPARATION. In a large bowl, combine three overflowing tablespoons of local honey with a cup (125 g) of powdered sugar and a cup (250 ml) of boiling milk. You need quite a strong, fragrant honey; a honey from Haute-Provence would be perfect. Gradually incorporate three cups (375 g) of all-purpose flour and a teaspoon of baking powder, and stir with a wooden spoon until you have a smooth batter. Beat in three whole eggs, 1/3 cup (100 g) melted butter and a large teaspoon of dried thyme leaves. Pour the batter into a well-buttered cake pan and bake in a medium oven (350°F/180°C) for 45 minutes. Unmold and let it cool completely on a cake rack, then wrap it in aluminum foil. Honeycake keeps for several days and is better eaten the day after it has been made.

Thyme-Scented Pear Preserve
~

To make this preserve—which tastes just as good when spread on toast for breakfast as it does served with cream cheese as a dessert—you will need fairly ripe, yet firm, juicy, fragrant pears. Peel the pears and discard the hard core containing the seeds. Slice the fruit into thin slices and weigh them. Arrange the slices in a preserving pan or heavy-bottomed pan and cover them with powdered sugar. Use 6 cups (750 grams) powdered sugar for every 2 1/4 pounds (1 kg) of pears. Add the juice of a lemon and a teaspoon of fresh thyme leaves. Stir carefully with a wooden spoon, without breaking the pear slices.

Cook over low heat, counting 45 minutes from the moment the liquid boils, stirring from time to time. Do not skim the liquid until the end of the cooking time, otherwise you will skim off the thyme. Pour into prepared preserving jars.

Thyme Tea
~

Begin by scalding the teapot with boiling water. Empty it, then place one sprig of thyme per cup in the pot. For this delicate herb tea it is more important than for the preceding recipes to try to find wild thyme, fresh if possible.

Fill the pot with boiling water, cover it with the lid, and let the liquid infuse for a few minutes. Serve this tranquilizing tea, which is an aid to digestion, without sugar, or sweeten it with a little honey if made with wild thyme.

ROSEMARY

Rosemary is an evergreen, its long, fairly stiff stems creating a thick bush that can grow to over six feet in height. It has the same preference as thyme for dry, sunny slopes, and even likes rocky soil. The leaves are long and narrow, stiff and thick, and in spring the tips of the branches are covered in pale blue flowers. The whole plant is strongly aromatic and in folk medicine it is credited with stimulant and antispasmodic properties.

In the sixteenth century, rosemary made the fortune of a queen. Queen Elizabeth of Hungary popularized an Elixir of Youth and Beauty whose formula, she claimed, had been given to her by an angel. This magic potion was nothing more than a distillation of alcohol in which the queen had macerated rosemary flowers. "Hungary Water" enjoyed huge popularity throughout the whole of Europe for many years.

For our present purposes, rosemary is a precious aromatic for flavoring meat and fish. In combination with thyme, bay leaf, and marjoram, it is used to flavor ratatouille. However, the fragrance is strong, almost overwhelming, and very difficult to combine with other herbs as it has a tendency to dominate them. It should therefore be used in small quantities, with great caution and finesse.

Rosemary Vinegar

~

Pick a few leafy branches of rosemary on the hillside and slip them into a bottle while they are very fresh. Fill the bottle to the top with wine vinegar, so that it covers the herb. Seal the bottle and leave the contents to macerate for four to six weeks before using this deliciously fragrant vinegar in salads.

Steamed Shoulder of Lamb with Rosemary

~

I believe that this cooking method for lamb is Moroccan, as is the idea of combining the flavors of cinnamon and rosemary. It is a brilliant idea and the delicate aroma pervades the whole house even before it has imparted a delicious flavor to the shoulder of lamb. This very simple and economical recipe is a favorite with even the most demanding gourmets.

PREPARATION. You will need a bone-in shoulder of lamb. Have your butcher cut it into boned serving pieces for you. Fill the bottom half of a couscous pot or steamer with branches of rosemary. Add four sticks of cinnamon, then add enough hot water to come halfway up the sides of the pot; bring to the boil over a high heat.

When the water boils, add the pieces of lamb to the top half of the pot and cover tightly so that they cook in the steam. Cook for about an hour. The aroma of the rosemary and cinnamon should be sufficient flavoring but if you insist on salt, salt the meat lightly just before serving.

Serve this delicately flavored meat accompanied by spelt grains cooked in salted boiling water for 30 minutes with about ten peeled and chopped garlic cloves.

Drain the grains then sprinkle them with a little olive oil from Haute-Provence.

This delicious dish should be accompanied by a Côtes-du-Luberon with its strong flavors of the *garrigue*, such as the Claude-Brasseur Cuvée '93 from the Citadelle at Ménerbes, although the Cuvée du Gouverneur '94 will do just as well.

Lamb Kabobs with Rosemary
~

In this recipe, as for the Bay Tree Twig Soup (see p. 108), it is the wood of the plant that supplies the flavor and fragrance. For six people, you will need a dozen freshly picked, wild or cultivated rosemary branches about 1 foot (30 cm) long. Strip off the leaves, reserving them for the marinade.

A few hours before cooking the kabobs, make a marinade from five tablespoons of

The two legs of lamb roasting on a spit are basted from time to time with a rosemary branch dipped in olive oil.

olive oil, the rosemary leaves, a few turns of freshly ground black pepper—do not add salt to the marinade, it should be added only when cooking is complete—and about 3 1/3 pounds (1.5 kg) boned and cubed shoulder of lamb. The cubes should be about the size of a walnut—allow 4–5 ounces (120–150 g) meat per skewer. Pour the marinade over the meat and mix well. Marinate for at least three hours, then spear the meat on the rosemary branches.

Prepare a barbecue, preferably with grapevine cuttings, but if they are unobtainable regular barbecue charcoal will do. From here onward, the success of the recipe depends upon the talents of the barbecue chef, and men are alleged to excel at this task. As for the cooking time, that depends on individual taste. Serve the kabobs immediately, while still smoking, accompanied by a cold ratatouille or a little garlic-flavored salad, and a few spoonfuls of leek preserve (see p. 71).

The rounded, peppery flavor of a Côtes-du-Rhône '96 from the Domaine de Gramenon, with its pronounced berry fruit flavor, will make this simple yet tasty dish into something sublime.

Godfather Bertrand's French Toast Cake

~

Crumble about one pound (500 g) of day-old bread into a large bowl. Add 1/3 cup (100 g) butter, cut into small pieces, 2/3 cup granulated sugar, and 3 tablespoons of ground cinnamon. Sprinkle with three pieces of grated, dried orange zest and the equivalent of a teaspoon of rosemary. Do not be surprised at the small quantity of rosemary; it should be present, but not overwhelming.

Scald a quart (1 liter) of milk and pour it over the bread. Stir the mixture, crushing any remaining lumps of bread with a wooden spoon. Finally, add four well-beaten eggs and stir again.

Turn into a buttered cake pan. Combine 4 tablespoons (50 g) of granulated sugar, 2 1/2 tablespoons (40 g) softened butter, and two well-beaten eggs, and spread the surface of the cake batter with this mixture. Bake for one hour in a gentle oven (300°F/150°C). Unmold and leave to cool.

Lovely Clara's Rosemary-Scented Crème Brûlée

~

Clara is a beautiful, tall, slender blonde who looks like the mysterious heroine of an American thriller. To our great joy, she adores food and is an exceptionally good cook. She is always inventing new and felicitous combinations of flavors and textures, manipulating aromatics, herbs, and spices with as much daring and talent as the most gifted young chefs. Our friend Clara often treats us to this sensational rosemary-scented crème brûlée.

PREPARATION. Bring a pint (500 ml) of light cream and a pint (500 ml) of milk to the boil with five or six rosemary sprigs. Remove from the fire and leave to infuse until it cools. Meanwhile, vigorously beat eight or nine egg yolks with five tablespoons of honey until you have a pale, smooth mixture. Combine the egg yolk mixture with the milk and pour this custard into a wide, shallow baking dish. Ideally, the custard should be no deeper than 1 inch (2.5 cm). Place the baking-dish in a pan of warm water and bake in a preheated gentle oven (300°F/150°C) for at least 45 minutes.

Remove from the oven and leave to cool completely before refrigerating. Chill for at least three hours before serving.

Just before serving, wipe the surface of the custard with paper towels, then sprinkle it with a very thin layer of granulated sugar. Then all you have to do is use a chef's blowtorch to caramelize the sugar. The great chefs all use the blowtorch method—trying to caramelize it under a grill will give a very poor result. It is quite easy to find a cook's blowtorch that uses small gas canisters. (Old-fashioned iron implements used for caramelizing exist, but they are very difficult to manipulate.)

Serve immediately, because the best thing about this dish is the contrast between the very cold, creamy custard and the hot, crunchy caramel.

SAGE

Sage was the "sacred herb" of the Romans, one to which all virtues were attributed. In Provence it is the main ingredient of the "life-saving" dish called *aigo boulido*, literally "boiled water." This bread and garlic soup is strongly flavored with sage, which gives it a powerful fragrance and numerous tonic, stimulating, stomachic, anti-spasmodic, anti-sweat, and fever–reducing properties.

The botanical name for sage, *Salvia officinalis*, is derived from the Latin *salvare* "to save, to cure." Legend has it that the plant saved the life of the baby Jesus, when the Virgin Mary hid her son in a sage bush to protect him from Herod's soldiers, who were under orders to kill all male newborn babies.

This lovely, perennial shrub has grayish-green, velvety leaves and flowers of the intense blue that Nature uses so sparingly. It prefers a dry, arid limestone soil. Sage is strongly aromatic and is best combined with meats such as lamb, mutton, or pork, or with fish. It also goes very well with chestnuts and dried pulses. Certain families in the Vaucluse area use sage to flavor the watermelon preserve they call "Meravillo" meaning "Marvel."

Sage-Leaf Fritters

~

I "stole" this sophisticated recipe from my friend Elisabeth Bourgeois who serves it at her restaurant, *Le Mas Tourteron*, in Gordes. These fragrant little fritters are delicious with an apéritif or cocktail, but I also serve them as an accompaniment to a leg of lamb or pork roast.

PREPARATION. Start by making a very light batter by pouring 1 cup (125 g) of sifted all-purpose flour into a bowl. Add a pinch of salt, a whole egg, and two tablespoons of olive oil. Mix this batter well, then dilute it by gradually adding 1/3 cup (100 ml) of ice water. Whisk an egg white into stiff, snowy peaks and gently fold it into the batter.

Choose about thirty freshly picked sage leaves. Dip them into the batter then sauté on both sides in hot olive oil. Drain them for a few moments on absorbent paper towels. Sprinkle with salt and serve immediately.

Try substituting flat-leafed parsley or fresh coriander for the sage, and let me know the results.

The Sage Barbecue Baster

~

This barbecue baster is an indispensable instrument for any self-respecting barbecue chef. It is made from a short broomstick about 1 foot (30 cm) long, to which a tuft of fresh sage leaves is attached with kitchen string. The little broom is dipped in olive oil, flavored with a choice of ingredients: vinegar, salt, and pepper, or soy sauce and honey, or even garlic and fresh thyme. Use it to baste fish and meats as they cook on the grill.

Edith's Sage Pasta

~

Edith Mézard excels at embellishing the everyday, thanks to her thousand-and-one household secrets, such as perfumed water for sprinkling on bed linen when ironing or how to embroider table linen with delicate patterns. This sage pasta is one of her most delicious secrets.

PREPARATION. Boil a large quantity of salted water, then throw in about one pound (500 g) of penne noodles, and cook them *al dente*—no longer. Before draining the pasta, remove a ladle of the cooking water and keep it warm in a serving bowl. This will keep the pasta from being too dry, since the only seasoning will be a large handful of sage leaves. The leaves should be finely shredded, then slightly stiffened by tossing them in a frying pan with 3 tablespoons of Nyons olive oil for a few minutes over medium heat. Mix the burning-hot pasta and the sage leaves and serve immediately with a flask of Nyons olive oil, a mill of white peppercorns, and a bowl of grated Parmesan cheese.

This simple, incredibly delicious dish can be washed down with a bottle of Côtes-de-Ventoux or a high-spirited, fruity Côtes-de-Luberon.

Sage-Flavored Scaloppini

~

This light, tasty dish comes to us from Italy, but marries extremely well with a Provençal ratatouille as an accompaniment.

PREPARATION. You will need tiny veal medallions (scaloppini) the same size and shape as slices of salami; ask for paper-thin, almost transparent slices of Parma ham. Don't worry if these very thin slices tend to fall apart. Then go into the garden and pick a nice bunch of sage.

Place a sage leaf on each veal scallop and cover it like a film with a thin piece of Parma ham. As each scallop is finished, transfer it to a large platter; do not allow the scaloppini to overlap.

The best way to cook the scaloppini is by sautéing them in two large frying pans at the same time. In each pan, melt a scoop of butter—about 1/2 ounce (15 g)—in one tablespoon of olive oil. Arrange the scaloppini in the pans with the ham side

downward. Cook them for four minutes on each side. The heat should be high, but not too high or the butter will burn; if it is too low, the veal will be soggy.

When the meat is done, season it very lightly with salt, as the Parma ham is already salted, but be generous with the pepper. Arrange on a heated serving platter. Deglaze the pans with two tablespoons of balsamic vinegar and pour over the meat. Serve immediately.

With this scaloppini dish, I like to drink a white Côtes-du-Rhône—a silky, voluptuous Saint-Péray with its bouquet of white peaches, or a rich and heavily perfumed white Crozes-Hermitage from the Domaines Pochon.

Father Bruno's Sage Meatballs
~

Father Bruno is the most lovable "grouch" of our whole tribe. In fact, he is not much of a cook, but he has managed to bring this single recipe to perfection. Sometimes on a Sunday—it always happens at Sunday lunch—he takes over the kitchen and shuts himself in for the purpose of concocting it, in the greatest secrecy and with a great clattering of pots and pans, sighs and terrifying imprecations launched against the cat, the dog, and anyone else who is unwise enough to cross the threshold of the kitchen at that moment. It needed this book and the success of my previous books for him to reveal his secret recipe to me. Here it is.

PREPARATION. Begin by making the sauce. Peel and thinly slice two onions. Peel and remove the germ from 4 or 5 garlic cloves and chop them. Lightly brown the onion and garlic in olive oil in a Dutch oven or heavy-based pan over a low heat, so as not to burn the garlic. When the onions begin to soften and turn golden, add 3 1/3 pounds (1.5 kg) of coarsely chopped ripe tomatoes. Naturally, these should be sun-ripened tomatoes, but when these are not available, canned tomatoes are preferable to the greenhouse variety. Add a bay leaf, two or three sage leaves, a sprig of thyme, a pinch of salt, a few turns of the pepper mill, and no fewer than five or six sugar lumps. Cover the pan and reduce the heat to as low as possible and let this tomato sauce simmer gently.

Meanwhile, lay a few slices of crumbled day-old bread in a bowl and pour one cup (250 ml) milk over them. Leave the bread to absorb the milk for a few minutes, then add 8 ounces (250 g) ground sausage, 8 ounces (250 g) ground veal, and 8 ounces (250 g) ground mutton or lamb. In the bowl of your food processor, grind a garlic clove with a large handful of freshly picked sage. Add this to the meat mixture. Add two whole eggs, salt, and pepper and mix well. Then shape it into meatballs with moistened hands.

When all of the meatballs are made, sauté them in a frying pan of hot olive oil until they color. As soon as each meatball is lightly browned, transfer it to the pan, and cook the meatballs in the tomato sauce for at least 30 minutes. Serve them with fresh pasta and grated cheese or with polenta (see p. 128).

Enjoy a sprightly young Cairanne, from the Domaine Marcel-Richaud for example, which should be slightly chilled to bring out its berry fragrances.

SAVORY

Savory—or rather, "savories," because there are two varieties—should be picked in early summer and dried and stored whole, away from air and light. The powdered savory sold commercially has usually lost all of its fragrance, which is a pity because home-picked savory has a delicate and subtle aroma.

The first of the two types of savory is Garden or Summer Savory (*Satureia hortensis*), an annual, with long, soft, dark green, pointed leaves, that flowers in late summer and has small pale pink blooms. Despite its name, it grows wild in the hills of Provence. The other type is Mountain or Winter Savory (*Satureia montana*), known in Provence as *pèbre d'ase* or *poivre d'âne* (donkey pepper) that also grows wild but is a perennial. The leaves are smaller and it has more leathery and branching, woody stems. Both types of savory are powerfully aromatic and have similar fragrances, perfect as flavor enhancers, in the way of salt. In Provence they are almost inseparable from goat's cheese.

The medicinal properties of savory are very similar to those of thyme, but several classical authors highlighted its aphrodisiac properties, claiming that its botanical name derived from the satyr, half-man half-goat, always lustfully chasing women and partaking in this herb so useful to his passions. The truth is that *satureia* means "stew," which leads us straight to the culinary arts.

Jeanne's Potatoes Stuffed
with Goat's Cheese

~

My daughter Jeanne serves us this delicious potato dish which has changed over the years at the whim of its creator, but which I am presenting today in its ultimate, most sublime form.

PREPARATION. Choose a dozen potatoes of the same size, so that they cook evenly, and without a blemish, since they will be served whole in their skins. Wash them and steam them for about 20 minutes. Meanwhile, cut up a slice of lean salt pork or, better still, *pancetta*, into little cubes and crumble a few savory sprigs. When the potatoes are cooked, that is to say, when the point of a knife penetrates them easily, slice off a lengthwise cap about 1/2 inch (1 cm) thick. Scoop out the potato flesh, being careful not to pierce the skin. With a fork mash the scooped-out potato and the flesh from their caps with five little fresh goat's cheeses and five tablespoons of olive oil. Add the tiny cubes of pork and the savory leaves, and half a minced garlic clove. Sprinkle generously with pepper but do not add salt because of the salty pork. Generously fill each potato with this stuffing and arrange them in an ovenproof dish.

Sprinkle with a little olive oil before baking for 15 minutes in a preheated hot (400°F/200°C) oven.

With this simple tasty country dish, I recommend a seductive white such as the powerful, yet fruity, Les Terrasses from the Mas de Daumas Gassac, as the ideal accompaniment.

Warm Pink Bean Salad

~

This summer salad is made with rosecoco beans, the same pink beans used to prepare the famous Provençal soup known as Soupe au Pistou, and with the mild, elongated little onions called shallots which Parisians call *cuisses de nymphe* (nymph's thighs). The other important ingredient is savory, of course. If you cannot get rosecoco beans, use pinto or California pink beans.

PREPARATION. Shell 2 1/4 pounds (1 kg) of pink beans. Peel a shallot and dice it. Put both into a saucepan with a bunch of savory. Cover with water and bring to a boil. Reduce the heat and cook at a very low boil for 45 minutes. Do not add salt until the cooking is finished.

Meanwhile clean six squid about 6 inches (15 cm) long; rinse and dry them. Slice the bodies into rings about 1/4 inch (5 mm) wide and fry along with the heads and tentacles in olive oil in a frying pan over high heat.

Make an *aïoli* (garlic mayonnaise) by crushing a garlic clove in a marble mortar and adding an egg yolk and a pinch of coarse salt. Exchange the pestle for a whisk to beat the mixture as you gradually add a thin stream of olive oil.

Finely chop a small handful of savory leaves and slice a large pink shallot into rings. Drain the still-warm beans and combine them with the squid in a bowl. Add the *aïoli* and toss lightly. Sprinkle with the shallot rings and the chopped savory.

Serve the salad immediately with a lively, refreshing young rosé wine. One of my favorites is the Château Pradeaux Bandol Rosé.

Fresh Broad Beans and Lamb Stew
with Savory

~

Savory is traditionally cooked with broad beans as well as with other legumes, not merely for its delicate perfume but also for its calming effects on these "creators of intestinal tornadoes." It is therefore the ideal flavoring for this spring stew.

PREPARATION. First shell 2 1/4 pounds (1 kg) of fresh beans. Make a court-bouillon with three quarts (3 liters) of water seasoned with salt and pepper, a carrot, an onion, and a bouquet garni consisting of parsley, fresh savory, a bay leaf and a piece of dried orange zest. Cook the beans in it for 20 minutes.

In a heavy-based casserole or Dutch oven, heat some olive oil and sauté 2 1/4 pounds (1 kg) of lamb cubes cut from the neck and breast. Cook the meat over low heat, stirring it frequently, for about 20 minutes. Drain the beans and remove their rather tough skins. Add them to the lamb with two unpeeled garlic cloves, which you have slightly crushed on the table with the palm of your hand, a small bunch of fresh savory leaves, a little water, salt, and a few grinds of the pepper mill. Cover and simmer gently for another 40 minutes.

Serve ten minutes after you have turned off the heat, accompanied by a supple wine—a Rasteau Côtes-du-Rhône from the Domaine de la Soumade whose fruitiness, elegance, and peppery notes are a lively accompaniment to this lamb stew.

JUNIPER

Should juniper have been included, alongside thyme and sage, in this book of sweet herbs?

Juniper is not exactly an herb, since the only part of the tree that is used are the berries that turn bluish-black when ripe, which happens in October or November of the third year after planting. The berries are harvested in almost the same way as olives and walnuts: a cloth is placed on the ground and the branches, with their painfully spiny leaves, are beaten with sticks. In the valley of the Ubaye, the berries were once actually picked from the branches by workers wearing thick lamb's-wool or rabbit-fur gloves. Juniper berries have long been known to be a powerful diuretic and tonic and are also famous for their remarkable aromatic qualities.

It is true that this shrub can be found far north of Provence and that its berries are better known for flavoring an Alsatian sauerkraut or Dutch gin than for their use in Provençal cooking. Yet the juniper bush flourishes on the hillsides here, sometimes confused with its relative, the prickly cedar or cade (*Juniperus oxycedrus*) which is very much a local tree and whose berries are larger and browner. Provençal hunters would be disappointed if they did not return from the hunt with a pocketful of the blue-black berries with which to flavor a rabbit stew.

Braised Chicken Livers with Juniper

~

Ideally, this salmis should be prepared in the spring, so that a few fresh morel mushrooms can be included in it, but if that is not possible, two or three dried morels can be substituted. If you use dried mushrooms, soak them in a bowl of warm water for an hour before starting to cook.

PREPARATION. Begin by finding a large frying pan in which to successively brown each ingredient in a little olive oil, before chopping them all together. Remove the outer skins of two large well-washed leeks and cut them into small pieces. Brown them gently over a low heat, then put aside in a large bowl. Replace the leeks with 7 ounces (200 g) of diced bacon and when the bacon is brown and crunchy, add it to the leeks. Add a little olive oil to the pan and when it is hot but not burning, throw in 2 1/4 pounds (1 kg) of washed and trimmed chicken livers. Stir constantly for 10 minutes, then add to the bowl.

Now cook the morels in the same way. Finish by adding a large lettuce, carefully washed and spun dry, which you should chop coarsely in the pan. It will sweat but will only begin to color when the water has evaporated. Add the braised lettuce leaves to the bowl with no fewer than ten crushed blue, i.e. ripe, juniper berries, salt, a few turns of the pepper mill, and four tablespoons of raspberry vinegar.

Mix all these ingredients well, then chop them up together, but not too finely, the salmis should retain the character of a peasant dish—it should not turn into a cream. Season to taste, and serve this delicious salmis as an appetizer or summer buffet dish, with large, warm slices of whole-wheat toast, accompanied, for example, by wild leek preserve (see p. 71). The dish can be eaten warm or cold, but never ice-cold.

A well-structured wine is needed to accompany the salmis—the red Coudoulet de Beaucastel, a Châteauneuf-du-Pape, which has a wonderfully fruity fragrance, is perfect.

Angèle's Chicken
with Juniper-Flavored Stuffing
~

Angèle is tall, beautiful, and generous. She runs her world—her cats, her dogs, her children, and her home—with the military precision of a two-star general, combined with the angelic sweetness of the Christmas Madonna. And of course, she is a wonderful cook.

PREPARATION. Choose a young, free-range, grain-fed chicken with giblets, weighing about 3 1/3 pounds (1.5 kg). Grind the chicken liver with 6 ounces (150 g) of veal and 3 ounces (100 g) of lean pork. Crush about ten juniper berries. Mix this stuffing with a whole egg, the juniper berries, a good pinch of salt, and a few grinds of the pepper mill. Line the cavity of the chicken with fresh sage leaves before inserting the stuffing.

Sew up the orifice with a large-eyed needle and truss the bird with kitchen string. Roast the chicken in a hot oven (400°F/200°C) for about 45 minutes, basting it with its own juices using the sage barbecue baster described on page 34, dipped in an olive oil that is not too fruity.

Accompany this roast chicken with a supple and aromatic wine such as Alain Graillot's Crozes-Hermitage, in which berry fruits predominate and which has a lovely roundness in the mouth.

Juniper Jam
~

Although it is quite a difficult recipe to get right, I must mention this mysterious and dark preserve, which is deep violet, almost inky black in color. It is a traditional delicacy of the Valley of the Ubaye and is used to accompany ham or is served with a little fresh goat's cheese as a dessert.

Although usually homemade for family consumption, it can be bought in the street markets in and around Barcelonette in the fall.

PREPARATION. First collect the juice of the juniper berries. To do this, cook the berries in water for two hours until they are soft enough to be crushed with the fingers. You will need five quarts (5 liters) of water for every 6 1/2 pounds (3 kg) juniper berries. Leave them to cool, then strain the liquid through a sieve, crushing the berries with a pestle. Pour the liquid thus obtained into a large pan and simmer over low heat until it thickens into a syrup.

Some people add sugar to the liquid, but that is not necessary. Pour it into prepared preserving jars. It keeps for a very long time, turning darker through the months and years.

FENNEL

The tall, slender, blue-green stems, lacy network of leaves, and large yellow umbels are so elegant! The aerial bouquets of fennel line paths and roadways in summer. I hesitated, however, before including it in this chapter because it is an inhabitant of the plains rather than the hills. Fennel is a stimulant and a stomachic; it is purgative and carminative. It was once noted for its property of stimulating the flow of milk in nursing mothers. Fennel tea, "sweetened with a little green licorice root," was prescribed for mothers whose milk supply was inadequate.

In cookery, it displays its talents in full measure. Fennel is the inseparable companion of fish; its leaves and stems, fresh or dried, are used to infuse fish court-bouillon broth, bouillabaisse, and other fish soups, and to flavor broiled sea bass and red mullet. If the fronds and stems are thrown onto the embers of a barbecue, they will impregnate it with their subtle fragrance. The tiny, chopped fresh leaves are delicious as a salad flavoring. Try it with potatoes. A little olive oil, salt, and a handful of chopped fennel leaves will taste delicious when sprinkled over waxy Pertuis potatoes, cooked in their skins, peeled, sliced into thick rounds, and served warm.

Cultivated fennel has large fleshy bulbs and is a delicious vegetable.

Malmousque Conger Soup

~

Malmousque is a small creek that runs through the heart of Marseille, right in front of the Château d'If, beside the valley of the Auffes. It is here that, a few years ago, I sampled this delicious soup at the home of friends. The conger eel is called *fielat* in Provence. Conger flesh is white, firm, and tasty. This is a bouillabaisse with a single fish ingredient—conger.

PREPARATION. Heat some olive oil in a Dutch oven or heavy-based pan. Chop an onion and add it to the pan with two crushed garlic cloves, two conger heads (which you can get from the fishmonger), a dozen sprigs of fennel, a piece of dried orange zest, and a small chopped chili pepper. Cook, stirring constantly, until the mixture begins to brown and stick to the pan. Pour in four quarts (4 liters) of boiling water. Add a large pinch of salt, cover the pan, and leave to simmer.

When the soup has been cooking for an hour, add some olive oil to another pan, and brown four or five leeks cut into rings,

Fennel bulbs are even better when cooked in fennel steam.

two coarsely chopped garlic cloves, four or five plump fennel bulbs, four tomatoes cut into quarters, a few dried fennel sprigs, and another piece of orange zest. Stir the mixture until it browns, then place a large sieve over the pan and add the entire contents from the first pan. Use a wooden pestle to crush the fish heads and vegetables, so as to extract as much liquid as possible. All that should remain in the sieve is a dryish paste that is to be discarded. Then add four large, waxy potatoes, washed, peeled, and sliced into rounds. Cook the soup at a rolling boil for about 10 minutes, before adding six to eight thick slices of conger to it. Continue

to cook the soup at a rolling boil for 10 minutes. Add a few threads of saffron just before you turn off the heat. I prefer to use saffron pistils, a pinch is enough. Remove and discard the fennel branches. Stir carefully, making sure the potatoes or conger do not fall to pieces, and serve immediately, accompanied with croutons made of day-old bread rubbed with garlic and a bowl of grated Gruyère cheese.

The best wine to serve with this conger soup is a white Cassis with floral aromas that is both ample and exciting, such as the Clos Sainte-Magdeleine, the best of the appellation.

Fennel and Celery Root with Steamed Fennel

~

This is a marriage made in heaven, an absolute delight, very simple, light, and extremely easy to prepare. Fill the bottom of a couscous pot or steamer with fresh or dried fennel sprigs until it is half full. Cover them with water and bring to the boil. Wash and peel a large celery root and slice it into six or eight pieces. Wash several plump fennel bulbs, discarding the outer layer. Slice them in half if they are

very big. Place the fennel bulbs and celery root in the top of the couscous pot or steamer, cover, and cook for 45 minutes in the fennel vapor. Serve with a little sea salt and olive oil on the table, to accompany broiled fish or roast meats. Personally, I love to use this as a vegetable with roast beef.

Fennel Oil
~

It is traditional in Provence to cook fennel on Michaelmas, the 29th of September, when it is seeding and is then at its best. Ideally, this delicious oil should be prepared at that time. Find an attractive bottle and fill it with branches of fennel with their leaves and a few umbels that are in flower or have run to seed. Cover the fennel with good quality olive oil, until it is totally submerged. Seal it with a cork and leave it for four weeks for the herb to infuse the oil. Replace the cork with a pouring spout and put it on the table every time you serve broiled fish or jacket potatoes, for example.

LAVENDER

Lavender, the queen of the herbs of Provence, has become the number one symbol of the region, illustrated in magazines throughout the world in its stunning purple-blue robe, sometimes depicted against a background of ancient olive trees or topped by a brilliant sunflower. It is a cliché, if ever there was one, for Provençal imagery, known and sold mainly for its essence and perfume. When you take a stroll along the roads of Haute-Provence, you will surely be intrigued by the strange, rather ugly, rusty, corrugated iron sheds that stand beside the rivers. These are lavender distilleries, used only during the short flowering period every year, and abandoned in the interval.

Lavender is known for its antispasmodic and diuretic properties. It once occupied a prominent place in folk medicine but was never used as a flavoring in cookery, however, until its recent media success inspired a few young, creative, and daring chefs to try and tame it in their recipes.

Frozen Lavender Nougat
with Lavender Honey

~

The recipe begins with the making of a custard. Vigorously beat nine egg yolks with five tablespoons of lavender honey until the mixture is clear and smooth. Combine two cups (500 ml) of whole milk with two cups (500 ml) of light cream and bring to a boil. Leave to cool for 10 minutes then pour it into the egg yolks, beating constantly with a wire whisk.

Cook the custard over a medium heat, stirring constantly until it coats the back of a spoon. Leave it to cool down, stirring occasionally. Then add 2/3 cup (150 g) pine nuts (pignolas), 1/3 cup (100 g) finely diced candied melon, and a small handful of freshly picked and crumbled lavender flowers. All that remains is to freeze this nougat in an ice-cream maker.

Clara's Lavender
Ice Cream

~

The recipe begins in the same way as the Frozen Lavender Nougat. Vigorously beat nine egg yolks with 3/4 cup (180 g) of granulated sugar until the mixture is smooth and pale. Combine two cups (500 ml) of whole milk with two cups (500 ml) of light cream. Add two handfuls of freshly picked lavender flowers. Pour the

mixture into a saucepan and bring to the boil. Remove it from the heat and leave to infuse for ten minutes. Strain the liquid and pour it over the egg yolk mixture. Return to the heat and cook, stirring constantly, until the custard coats the back of a spoon. Leave it to cool completely before freezing the mixture in an ice-cream maker.

DANDELION

The French name for dandelion, *pissenlit* (wet-the-bed), clearly illustrates its diuretic properties. It is also the perfect salad ingredient for those who lack appetite, whose digestion is poor, or who suffer from liver problems. All will benefit from this common herb with its dentate leaves, arranged in a ring around the tall stalks topped by a golden yellow flower, which upon maturity turns into a gossamer ball of fluffy, silky umbrellas that carry away the seeds on the wind. In the old days in France, just as young girls would play "he-loves-me, he-loves-me not" with daisy petals, they would blow the dandelion seed-head to see how many years they would wait for their wedding day. The number of times they had to puff represented the number of years in question. If the seeds rose heavenward, happiness was assured, but if they fell downward it was better to start over on the next day when there might be more wind! The little bald knob on the end of the stem, which remained when the seeds had blown away, gave the dandelion its Old French name of *tête de moine* (monk's head).

The dandelion is known for being a delicious ingredient in a salad of wild herbs. But dandelion flowers, infused and cooked like jam with sugar, also make an exquisite jelly, so similar in color and flavor to certain types of honey as to almost be mistaken for them.

Dandelion Flower Preserve

~

Go down to the fields in spring, when the dandelions are in flower, taking a large basket, and pick exactly three hundred and fifty dandelion flowers. When you get home, wash the flowers in plenty of running water under the faucet, taking care to discard any recalcitrant insect hiding in the thicket of petals. Drain the flowers, spread them out to dry, and leave them for twenty-four hours. On the following day, bring three pints (1.5 liters) of water to the boil with the juice of one orange and one lemon in a large pan. Add the flowers. Extinguish the heat, cover the pan, and let the liquid infuse until it is completely cold. Filter the juice, weigh it, and add the same weight of sugar. Simmer this mixture in a preserving pan or heavy-bottomed pan for about forty minutes, or until it is the consistency of liquid honey. Pour it into jars.

Spice Cake with Dandelion Jelly and Orange

~

Dandelion jelly is so similar to honey in texture and flavor that it can very easily replace honey in a cake such as this. It has its own personality, however, so it is worth trying this recipe.

PREPARATION. In a large bowl, mix three overflowing tablespoons of dandelion jelly with one cup (250 g) of sugar and a cup of boiling milk. Then gradually add two cups (250 g) of all-purpose flour, one cup (125 g) of rye flour, and one teaspoon of baking powder. Stir with a wooden spoon until you have a smooth batter. Beat in three whole eggs, 1/3 cup (100 g) melted butter, and a tablespoon of orange peel cut into very thin strips. Pour the batter into a well-buttered cake pan and then bake it for forty-five minutes in a medium-hot oven (350°F/180°C). Unmold it and leave it to cool completely on a cake rack. Serve this spice cake at tea-time or as a snack, sliced, and with a pot of fresh butter.

Dandelion Salad

~

The dandelion has always been harvested for the little evening salad, a feast for Sunday strollers. Bitter and sometimes a little tough—exactly why some people like it—it is preferable to pick dandelions in early spring, and to do so along out-of-the-way paths rather than by polluted roadsides. Choose young shoots that are milder and more tender than those on the large summer dandelions. The buds are also delicious in salads. The bitter flavor of the dandelion improves if a little garlic is added to a vinaigrette dressing. Unlike other green salads, it is best heavily seasoned rather than merely sprinkled with olive oil, even a fruity one.

In Lyon, mustard is added to the dressing, as well as a few browned bacon bits and a coddled egg—an egg cooked for slightly longer than a soft-boiled egg, about six minutes, then carefully shelled so that it remains whole.

In Aups, in the upper Var valley, dandelion salad dressing consists of a mixture of ground walnuts and anchovy fillets coarsely ground in a mortar with a little olive oil.

Everywhere else in Provence, the salad is served with an olive oil vinaigrette, laced with fried croutons rubbed with garlic cloves to make them glisten.

POPPY SHOOTS

Monsieur and Madame Hector are greengrocers who have a market stall in my home village of Isle-sur-la-Sorgue. Every spring for years, they have been selling delicious greens with a slightly peppery flavor which they call "wild spinach" and which I eventually identified to my great surprise as being young poppy shoots.

This annual plant invades the crops and surrounding areas in late spring with its glorious red flowers, whose petals are as thin and papery as chiffon. Herbalists use only the petals and dried seed capsules for their tranquilizing, soporific, and pectoral properties. The wild poppy is from the same family as the opium poppy and mildly reproduces its effects.

In Germany, Austria, and northern Europe, poppy seeds are used in baking and patisseries. I once tasted a wonderful couscous in southern Morocco that contained poppy buds. But in Provence, the young shoots and leaves are cooked just like spinach or chard. However, the green part of the poppy gives the dish a special flavor that is clean, stronger than that of green chard leaves and more peppery than spinach.

Poppy Shoots
with Anchovies
~

Wash, sort, and drain three large handfuls of poppy or spinach leaves, a nice round butter lettuce, a handful of rocket plant, and a young leek. Chop them all coarsely.

Heat some olive oil in a heavy-bottomed frying pan and cook six or seven anchovy fillets. Add the chopped herbs, two bay leaves, and about 20 black olives. Mix well and cover the pan. Cook for about 20 minutes, stirring from time to time. Sprinkle with a little olive oil at the time of serving.

Serve hot to accompany an entrée or cold as an appetizer.

Sweet Poppy
Shoot Tart

~

This surprising and delicious dessert is one of many versions of the traditional Nice chard tart.

PREPARATION. Wash and sort two large handfuls of young poppy shoots and leaves or chard leaves. Discard any tough stems but keep the flower buds. Blanch the greens in boiling water for five minutes then drain them as thoroughly as possible.

Rinse 2/3 cup (100 g) yellow raisins (sultanas) in a sieve. Soak them in three tablespoons of rum.

Make a short-crust dough by quickly combining two cups (250 g) all-purpose flour, a pinch of salt, 1/4 cup (50 g) butter, three tablespoons olive oil and three tablespoons of water. Roll out the dough to fit a buttered pie tin or tart pan. Prick the bottom with a fork and bake alone in a moderate (350°F/170°C) oven for 20 minutes. The crust should not color.

Meanwhile, in a bowl, mix two egg yolks, 2/3 cup (100 g) of thick crème fraîche, six tablespoons (75 g) sugar and the grated rind of an untreated lemon.

Remove the crust from the oven and spread the poppy leaves over it. Sprinkle it with the soaked sultana raisins and 2/3 cup (100 g) pine nuts (pignolas). Finally pour the custard mixture over the tart and return it to the oven. Bake for another 20 minutes. Remove it from the oven and let it cool completely before sprinkling it with powdered sugar.

Serve with a well chilled Beaumes-de-Venise. The wine of the Muscat appellation that I recommend is the Beaumes-de-Venise '95, a particularly good year, with its fragrances of candied orange and lemon, and its unique fruity concentration.

NETTLES

There are several types of nettle, including the Greater Nettle, the Roman Nettle, and the Stinging Nettle, and they are among the least favorite herbs. There is good reason for this. Not only do they violently attack anyone unwise enough to pick them without wearing a thick pair of gloves—they even sting unprotected legs when you walk past them—but in their bitter fight against man since time immemorial, they seem to flourish on man's misfortune, growing on his rubbish and his ruins. The nettle is the perfect example of a weed that is actually much better than you might think, once you know how to pick it. Not only does it have curative properties—it has been used for centuries for tending wounds and for its purifying properties—but it is also delicious to eat. Nettles are made into delightful soups by cooking them like sorrel or watercress. They can even be used to replace spinach with the advantage that once cooked they turn a brilliant emerald green. On the other hand, since it is hard to find them in the heart of the city, they can easily be replaced by spinach.

Nettle Omelet
~

Put on some thick gloves and pick about twenty young nettle shoots. Do not worry, cooking totally destroys their irritant properties. Wash the leaves and discard the stems. Dry them on paper towels.

Thinly slice an onion and gently sauté it in a little olive oil in a frying pan over a low heat, stirring from time to time. Add all the nettle leaves at once, along with a peeled and coarsely chopped garlic clove. Season with salt and pepper.

Increase the heat slightly and continue to stir with a wooden spoon until the nettles have wilted. This should happen quite quickly. Remove the pan from the heat.

Break eight or nine eggs into a bowl and season them with salt and pepper. Beat them lightly, just enough to combine the yolks and whites. Add a little olive oil to the frying pan and pour the beaten egg and herb mixture into it. The omelet should be cooked over low heat, so that it does not toughen. Fold it in two and serve while it is still runny in the center.

It is difficult to choose a wine for an omelet but I would recommend a white Côteaux-d'Aix, especially a powerful, very floral one such as a Château Calissanne.

Salt Cod with Nettles

~

The night before you intend to cook the salt cod, soak it in a large bowl, changing the water several times to remove the excess salt. Then poach the cod in water that is barely simmering, never letting it come to the boil. Drain the cod and leave it to cool, before carefully removing the skin and bones, and flaking it.

Blanch a large quantity of nettles in a pot of boiling water. They wilt like spinach and reduce considerably. Drain well in a sieve and chop them finely.

Chop an onion finely and brown it lightly in olive oil in a large frying pan over a low heat. Add two or three well-rinsed salt anchovy fillets and let them melt before you add the chopped nettle leaves. Sauté the mixture, stirring it with a wooden spoon. Add a little chopped garlic and ground pepper and possibly a little salt, but don't forget that the anchovies are salted.

Traditionally, this is all that is required, but I personally add one or two tablespoons of crème fraîche or heavy cream. I can assure you it doesn't spoil the dish. Pour half the nettle mixture into a well-oiled gratin dish and then add the flaked, poached cod. Cover with the rest of the nettles. Cover the dish with grated Gruyère cheese along with a few dry breadcrumbs and sprinkle with a little

olive oil. Place in a preheated moderate oven (350°F/180°C) to brown for at least 15 minutes.

Serve this dish piping hot with a Coudoulet Blanc '96, a Château de Beaucastel Côtes-du-Rhône with its well-developed bouquet and plenty of body. Or you could serve a white Château de Crémat, a strong Bellet (a wine from Nice) that is powerful and robust, combining a fullness in the mouth with light freshness.

WILD ASPARAGUS

Wild asparagus is a perennial of the Lilaceae family. It develops thick underground stems. In spring, it produces tender, edible young shoots before it ramifies into an infinity of little branches with soft, green spines. These large asparagus branches make it easy to find the young shoots that grow at their feet in bushes and hedgerows, on embankments, and at the foot of walls and trees. It is these young shoots that are worth picking, but they are sometimes difficult to find in the scrub, because they are very thin, much thinner than cultivated asparagus. The people of Provence love to go asparagus-picking and every spring they boast to their friends about the "blow-outs"—feasts of wild asparagus steamed and served with a vinaigrette dressing while still warm. It is probably this liking for wild asparagus that is the reason why in Provence, green cultivated asparagus is favored, that is to say asparagus that has been allowed to grow in the open air, so that the air and the sun has given that lovely purple-green color to the 8 inches (20 cm) of the spears. Elsewhere, asparagus is usually cultivated blanched, that is to say it is covered with a little mound of earth so that it remains completely white and colors only in those parts that are close to the surface. There are four types of asparagus—white, white-violet, violet, and the green, Provençal type. Traditionally, northern Europeans prefer their asparagus paler.

Wild Asparagus
with Light Sauce

~

When I was a child, I spent a lot of time in the kitchen watching my mother prepare the meal. I remember that one of her favorite comments was "Look, we'll put cream in this instead of butter. It will make it lighter!" Her idea of "light" cooking would make those who favor "0% fat" laugh today, but I happen to prefer my mother's type of cooking. This light mayonnaise contains olive oil without cream and it goes very well with asparagus, wild or otherwise.

PREPARATION. Blanch the wild asparagus in salted, boiling water for about 10 minutes, then drain and arrange it in an attractive serving dish. Naturally, you can also use thin, green, cultivated asparagus. Pour an egg yolk into a bowl, reserving the white. Add a small teaspoon of strong Dijon mustard and beat well, making a mayonnaise by gradually adding a thin stream of good olive oil. It is most important for the egg yolk, the mustard, and the oil to be at the same temperature. Whip the egg white into stiff peaks and gently incorporate it into the mayonnaise. Add the juice of a lemon and perhaps a little salt. Serve the mayonnaise in a sauceboat, alongside the asparagus.

Thanks to this smooth, fragrant sauce, the asparagus can be accompanied by a *vin jaune* from the Jura with its typical nutty flavor, served in a carafe at a temperature of 58°–60°F (15–16°C). Or try a white Arbois from the Savanien grape variety or, in a different register, a white Côtes-du-Rhône such as Saint-Joseph.

Lasagna with
Wild Asparagus

~

Blanch one pound (500 g) of wild asparagus or small green asparagus in plenty of boiling, salted water for about 10 minutes. Drain it and use a fork to remove and discard the tough part of the stem, at the base. Make a light béchamel sauce with six tablespoons (75 g) butter, melted in a small heavy-based pan. Add three tablespoons of all-purpose flour and mix well with the butter. Then add three cups (750 ml) cold whole milk all at once. Dissolve the flour in the milk using a sauce whisk. Then stir the mixture over the heat with a wooden spoon until the sauce thickens. Extinguish the heat. Salt lightly and pepper generously. Add a large tablespoon of crème fraîche.

Pour a ladle of sauce into the bottom of a buttered gratin dish and arrange the pieces of lasagna on top of it. (It is easy to find lasagna in the stores that does not require prior cooking, but I remember the days when one had to first boil the pasta, spreading it out on a large cloth to drain before filling it.) Distribute one third of the asparagus over the pasta. Sprinkle with grated cheese—for this recipe, I prefer Dutch cheese, such as an aged Gouda. Sprinkle with a ladle of sauce and repeat the operation, until all the asparagus has been used up. Finish with a layer of pasta. Pour the rest of the sauce over it as well as a little grated cheese.

Bake the lasagna for at least an hour in a preheated medium (350°F/180°C) oven. When the top looks as if it is browning nicely, reduce the heat to (300°F/150°C) and leave it to cook for a few minutes more.

I often make this dish using wild leeks or fresh garden peas, which I first sweat in olive oil with bacon bits and one or two pearl onions.

The wines chosen for the previous recipe go perfectly well with asparagus, but you could also accompany this gratin with a Château de la Nerthe, a white Châteauneuf-du-Pape, with its wonderful roundness and aromatic complexity.

WILD LEEKS

The wild leek, also known in Provence as *le poireau des vignes* (the vine leek) or *le poireaux des oliviers* (the olive-tree leek), emerges in spring in well-tilled soil in which it develops extremely well. It belongs to the same family as garlic, and its bulbous root is divided into little cloves that assure its reproduction. It looks very much like a smaller, thinner version of the cultivated leek. It has diuretic and slightly laxative properties and is recommended for dieters, but above all, it is a delicious vegetable. This "poor man's asparagus" is mainly served as an appetizer, boiled and accompanied by a vinaigrette dressing, but it can be used in a wide variety of delicious dishes as a substitute for garden leeks.

Leek Preserve
~

Remove the outer layer of skin from about twenty wild leeks and wash them carefully. Peel 1 pound (500 g) of new white onions. Coarsely chop the onions and leeks and add them to a large frying pan in which you have heated a little olive oil. Add 2/3 cup (100 g) yellow raisins (sultanas) and cook over low heat, stirring constantly with a wooden spoon, to ensure that the onions and leeks do not turn dark or the preserve will be disastrously bitter.

When the contents of pan are very lightly golden, pour a bottle of dry, white wine over it and simmer, uncovered, until the wine has almost completely evaporated. Leave to cool before serving.

This preserve makes an excellent accompaniment to cold meats. If you do not have wild leeks at your disposal try this recipe using the onions on their own.

Blanquette of Veal with Wild Leeks

~

Ask your butcher to cut 1 3/4 pounds (800 g) veal shank, ribs, or shoulder into large cubes. First freshen the veal by placing it in a saucepan, adding cold water to cover, and heating it to boiling point. Remove it from the fire and drain it.

In a stewpot, make a court-bouillon with 3 quarts (3 liters) water, seasoned with pepper and salt, a whole, scraped carrot, an onion spiked with three cloves, and a bouquet garni of parsley, a sprig of thyme, and one or two bay leaves. When the liquid boils, add the pieces of veal and simmer for 1 hour. Meanwhile, carefully sort and wash 2 1/4 pounds (1 kg) of wild leeks. If you do not have vineyards or olive groves nearby, or they are out of season, use cultivated leeks. Remove the outer skin and leave them whole, then tie them in a bunch with kitchen string. Once the veal has been cooking for an hour, add the bunch of leeks and simmer for another half-hour, counting from the moment the liquid returns to the boil.

To make the velouté sauce, take a heavy-bottomed pan and place 1/4 cup (60 g) butter and 2 tablespoons (30 g) flour in it. Heat, beating constantly, then add five ladles of liquid from the blanquette, beating with a sauce whisk to prevent lumps from forming. In a bowl, combine two egg yolks with one cup (250 ml) of crème fraîche or heavy cream. Add two tablespoons of the sauce and mix well before pouring it into the casserole, stirring constantly for one minute. Remove from the heat and taste before seasoning with salt and pepper. Add the juice of half a lemon and 1/8 teaspoon grated nutmeg.

Remove the string from the bunch of leeks. Arrange the veal slices and leeks in a shallow serving bowl, coat with the sauce, and serve the rest of the sauce in a sauceboat.

This blanquette will go very well with a white Côtes-du-Rhône, especially a Crozes-Hermitage from the Domaine des Entrefaux, which is ample in the mouth and has the aroma of honey.

Wild Leeks and Ham au Gratin

~

Wash and sort 2 1/4 pounds (1 kg) of wild leeks or young garden leeks. Cook them for 15 minutes in boiling, salted water, then drain them. Have cooked ham cut into ten thin slices. Lightly butter a gratin dish. Wrap little bunches of five or six leeks in a slice of ham and arrange the packet in the dish. In a bowl, combine one cup (250 ml) of crème fraîche or heavy cream with 7 ounces (200 g) grated cheese and coat each packet with this mixture. Sprinkle with a little freshly ground black pepper and bake in a preheated hot (450°F/230°C) oven for 15 minutes.

Here again, a white Côtes-du-Rhône would be perfect, but try this gratin with a fresh, ample aromatic rosé such as a Tavel from the Domaine de la Mordorée.

The Herb Garden and Herbs from the Garden

An herb garden does not need to be large. Planting the loveliest of gardens requires only some 30 square feet (10 square meters) in a sheltered, sunny spot or even on a balcony. It could be a magical thicket, a wonderful miniature forest— but this is a difficult design to achieve, requiring a very green thumb. It could be laid out like a formal garden, with beds of parsley and mint, facing patches of arugula and lemon balm, framed by rows of thyme, the corners punctuated by large pots of basil. To give a striking perspective, you could plant the borders with tall umbelliferous herbs, such as aniseed and fennel, surrounded by alternating bushes of sage and rosemary. Or why not a cottage garden, naïvely organized into small herbaceous beds bordering a path of tiny gray pebbles? The Latin name of each herb could be written on a little wooden stake planted beside it, and at the end of the path a row of nasturtiums would make the garden look as if it were in a state of perpetual celebration. A perfect choice, since nasturtium flowers are so delicious in salads!

Whatever type of garden you choose, it should contain all sorts of herbs—those that usually grow in gardens, but also all the wild ones, the tender shoots of the fields and fragrant herbs of the hills. Most of these wild herbs are quite easily "tamed" and both their seeds and young plants can be found in nurseries and garden centers.

BASIL

Provence owes much of its identity to India, including, of course, brightly colored cotton calico, printed with sprigs of exotic blooms, and indigo, the deep blue dye used for denim, originally *de Nîmes* (from Nîmes). One day, hidden among the bales of cotton cloth, the silks, sacks of spices, and other treasures imported from India, there arrived an herb that is considered sacred in its native country. A few centuries later, it has become the herb considered most typical of Provençal cooking—basil. In India, basil is dedicated to the god Vishnu who will not suffer the plant to be badly treated in any way and who rejects the prayers of those who destroy it. Curiously, these sacred legends also made their way to Provence. At one time, the picking of basil in Provence was accompanied by an intricate ritual. The herbalist had to purify his right hand, the one he used to pick the plant, by taking an oak branch and dipping it in the water of three different streams before sprinkling it over the hand. He had to wear clean clothes and distance himself from any impurity.

Today, basil is widely cultivated in various varieties. The commonest is "fine green basil" which the producers call "Marseillais." It grows in compact, round tufts which makes it particularly suited for growing in pots. But there are many other varieties including "purple," "large green," and "bush" basil. It is important to note that basil is best if eaten fresh. When dried it loses all its flavor and personality, and if preserved in oil its flavor is denatured. But you have the whole summer to enjoy the sight of a pretty pot of basil in the kitchen window.

Basil Purée

~

Peel 3 1/3 pounds (1.5 kg) of old potatoes. Cook them in boiling salted water for 20 minutes.

Meanwhile wash and wipe dry a large bunch of flat-leafed parsley and a large bunch of small-leafed basil. Remove the leaves from the stems and discard any stems that are too tough. Grind the leaves and soft stems in a food processor.

In a saucepan, warm 3/4 cup (200 ml) milk with 3/4 cup (200 ml) olive oil. When the potatoes are cooked, drain and mash them in a food mill or potato-masher. Mix the milk and oil with the potatoes, stirring with a wooden spoon, and finally add the herbs. Salt and pepper to taste and serve immediately. This purée makes a splendid accompaniment to fish.

Leek and Potato Pistou

~

Soupe au Pistou is indubitably one of the glories of Provençal cooking. It calls for lots of vegetables, such as onions, zucchini and potatoes, as well as green, white, and pink beans. Some people add tomatoes and pine nuts; others throw in pasta, carrots, or salt pork. In fact there are a thousand-and-one recipes for *soupe au Pistou* and almost all of them are delicious.

The recipe I am giving you here is a very old one from the area of Nice, and the result is lighter and simpler than other versions. Although the traditional beans are absent, it is a genuine Pistou, because the recipe begins with "crushing" and that is what "pistou" is all about. (The word comes from the Latin *pistus*, meaning "crushed" or "pounded.") So to begin you will need a marble mortar and a boxwood or olive-wood pestle with which to crush a bunch of large-leafed basil and three large Provençal garlic cloves in one cup (250 ml) of olive oil, reducing the mixture to a pulp.

The real difference is in the ingredients of this soup, which consist exclusively of leeks and potatoes, although a couple of white onions could be slipped in without too much harm.

So, after pounding the pistou, take a deep pot and fill it with two quarts (2 liters) of salted and peppered water. Take one pound (500 g) of potatoes, washed, peeled, and diced, and add them to the pot with one pound (500 g) of the white part of the leeks sliced into rings, and the two onions. The soup should cook for one hour. Remove it from the heat and mix it with the pistou (basil purée) immediately. Season to taste. Serve this wonderful soup with a large bowl of Parmesan shavings, which will melt around the soup vegetables.

To drink with this tasty soup, try a red wine from the Domaine de la Bernarde, with its smell of violets and truffles (in the case of the old vintages) and its voluptuous suppleness.

Should any soup be left over, add two tablespoons of crème fraîche or thick yogurt and purée in a blender, before chilling for an hour or two in the refrigerator. Garnish this cold soup with a few basil leaves and serve it ice-cold as a starter. There is no need for Parmesan when served cold.

Broiled Tuna Steak, Red Rice with Herbs, and Green Sauce

~

Here are three recipes in one, because I like the way they work together. Begin by preparing the herbed rice, starting a good hour beforehand. Red rice from the Camargue is a whole-grain, wild rice that is delicious and very nutritious. It needs slightly longer cooking than white rice. Boil three quarts (3 liters) of salted and peppered water in a deep pot. Add a garlic clove, two sage leaves, and a small sprig of thyme. Then pour in one pound (500 g) of Camargue red rice that has simply been rinsed in a colander under running water. Cook for 45 minutes. Stop the heat, cover the pot, and let the rice swell for another 30 minutes. Just before serving, remove the garlic clove and herbs, and drain the rice in a colander. Pour the rice into a serving bowl and sprinkle it with a little olive oil.

To prepare the Green Sauce, use a wooden pestle and a marble mortar to grind a pinch of coarse salt, a garlic clove, a handful of basil leaves, and a large handful of flat-leafed parsley leaves. When they have been reduced to a paste, add an egg yolk. Trade the pestle for a sauce whisk and gradually beat olive oil into the green sauce, as you would for a mayonnaise.

As for the tuna, you will need a large piece that is no less than 2 3/4 inches (6–7 cm) thick. Discard the skin and bone, and slice the tuna into as many steaks as you need. If you have a barbecue or grill, rub the tuna steaks with coarse salt, then grill them for four minutes on each side. You can also pan-fry the tuna. Sprinkle the heated, dry frying pan with a pinch of coarse salt and arrange the pieces of tuna on the salt. Cook for four minutes on each side. The surfaces that touched the pan should look reddish-brown, as if they were caramelized. The edges of the tuna steak should be uniformly white, leaving the fish with a pink center. Let me know how you like it!

Serve hot, accompanied by the Red Rice and Green Sauce.

PARSLEY

Parsley comes with flat or curly leaves. I shall only discuss the former, since it is infinitely tastier. For me, the latter is inseparably linked with the sinister and far-too-small pat of butter—wrapped in gold-colored paper and inflexible from having spent too much time in the refrigerator—surrounded by three black olives and used to "garnish" a vast array of cold cuts, spread out on a stainless-steel Louis XV platter.

In the wild, flat-leafed parsley bears a dangerous resemblance to another umbelliferous plant—hemlock. However, it is widely cultivated and sold everywhere, so you need not take the risk of picking the wrong plant while out for a walk. Parsley is well-known for its tonic, blood-purifying properties, its ability to reduce fever and increase blood flow; it is less well-known as a remedy for wasp- and bee-stings. Just crush a leaf between your fingers and apply the juice to the sting.

Parsley is a remarkable condiment that is used almost everywhere in the world. My mother never served a dish of vegetables, such as green beans, or a tomato salad, without generously sprinkling it, just before serving, with lots of chopped, flat-leafed parsley. And it was always my job to chop the parsley into a little mustard glass, using large kitchen scissors that my tiny child's hands had difficulty in manipulating.

Green Beans the Way My Mother Made Them

~

This is one of those perfectly simple family recipes that is so easy to make, it never shows up in a cookbook. Yet it is so delicious that I strongly advise you to hurry up and try it.

PREPARATION. Top and tail 2 1/4 pounds (1 kg) of freshly picked firm and crisp green beans. String them if necessary, then wash and drain. Bring three quarts (3 liters) of water to a boil in a big pot. Add a handful of coarse salt and three or four large onions, skinned and diced—but not too finely. Boil the onions for at least 15 minutes before adding the beans. What makes this dish so delicious is the contrast between the nearly melted onion and the firm almost *al dente* green beans. Cook the beans for about 10 minutes, depending on their size. Taste them and if they are cooked but still firm, pour the contents of the pot into a colander. Leave to drain.

Arrange the onions and beans in a serving platter. Dot with fresh butter or sprinkle with olive oil—both are delicious in their own way. Add the juice of half a lemon and a good handful of freshly picked, finely-chopped flat-leafed parsley.

Anchovies Terre-Salée Style
~

Terre-Salée is a lovely spot in the Camargues, not far from Saintes-Marie-de-la-Mer. There is a little white-walled cottage with bright blue shutters, a pond edged with bulrushes, a rowboat tied to a jetty, and the incessant ballet of egrets wheeling overhead. Here, at twilight on a long summer's day, my friend Mireille often treats us to these sublime anchovies, whose silvery tints almost disappear in the mass of luscious green parsley that accompanies them.

PREPARATION. Try to use salted anchovies for this recipe, as they are more pliable and tastier than anchovies canned in oil, even if more work to prepare. You first have to clean them, discarding the tail, fins, and bones, and then rinse them in running water. Place on absorbent paper to drain. For those in a hurry or simply too lazy, anchovies in oil may be used, but first rinse in cold water to which a little vinegar has been added. That will render them a bit more flexible.

For each pound (500 g) of anchovy fillets, you will need 3 or 4 bunches of flat-leafed parsley, 2 untreated lemons, and 2/3 cup (200 ml) olive oil from the valley of Les Baux. Do not be surprised by the quantities, since these anchovies are so delicious that, served with an aperitif such as a glass of pastis or a dry white wine and one or two fresh, crusty French loaves, you won't need to go to the trouble of making an appetizer.

Arrange the anchovy fillets in a shallow serving bowl. Cut the unpeeled lemons into thin slices. Remove the pips, then cut the slices into eighths and sprinkle them over the anchovies. Carefully cut the stems away from the parsley so as to leave only the leaves, and chop the leaves. Sprinkle the chopped parsley over the dish. In a bowl, mix the olive oil with two chopped garlic cloves, 1/8 teaspoon of Cayenne pepper, a teaspoon of sweet paprika, a teaspoon of ground cumin, and a few grinds of black pepper. Do not add salt, since the anchovies are salty. Pour this dressing over the anchovies. Cover the dish with plastic wrap and leave it to marinate for three hours before serving.

Serve with an aperitif, such as glass of Bardouin pastis or a dry white wine with the fullness, body, and strength of a Château de Crémat Bellet, and don't forget the two fresh baguettes.

Madame Zaza's Lemon-and-Parsley-Flavored Tabbouleh
~

When I was in Syria, I ate a delicious tabbouleh in which there was so much parsley and so little couscous that it was actually more of a raw parsley salad, flavored with lemon juice, decorated with scanty tomato slices for color contrast, then mixed with a few symbolic grains of couscous. This tabbouleh was a fine accompaniment to the little appetizers called *mezze*, which are served in the Middle East, such as chick-pea and sesame purée (humus), aubergine caviar (baba ganouche) and stuffed vine leaves (dolma). Personally, I prefer the following parsley-and-lemon tabbouleh that my friend, Madame Zaza, makes in midsummer, which emphasizes the couscous, that is swollen by soaking in lemon juice.

Anchovies Terre-Salée style.

The tabbouleh should be made a day in advance. Begin by peeling four untreated lemons, using a vegetable peeler or very sharp knife, making sure not to include the white part (pith) of the lemon, which is very bitter. This peel or zest should be translucent. It should then be sliced into very thin strips. Pour one pound (500 g) of medium-grain couscous into a large *tian* or ovenproof earthenware dish, with the juice of about 10 lemons. Add the lemon zests and mix carefully. Cover the couscous with a cloth and leave it to swell overnight.

On the following day, rub the couscous grains between your fingers to separate them. Finely chop a large quantity of flat-leafed parsley, enough to color the tabbouleh green. Mix the couscous with the chopped parsley and 1 cup (250 ml) of olive oil. Season with salt and pepper to taste.

Place the tabbouleh in the refrigerator for another hour or two before serving it with a well-structured rosé such as the pleasantly fruity Bandol from the Château Romasson (Domaines Ott).

Fried Parsley
~

For this recipe, as for the others, it is best to choose flat-leafed parsley as it is so much tastier than the curly-leafed variety. Remove the leaves from a bunch of parsley, leaving about 1/2 inch (1 cm) of stem on them. Heat the oil in a deep-fryer to 380°F (190°C) then throw in the parsley being careful to avoid the inevitable splattering of oil. Fry the parsley for four minutes, just long enough for it to become crunchy. Drain it and leave for a few moments on a sheet of absorbent paper towels. Sprinkle with a dash of table salt. Serve as a garnish for zucchini fritters or broiled fish.

CORIANDER

Coriander is sometimes known as Chinese parsley. The Chinese, as well as Indians, Egyptians, Hebrews, Greeks, and Romans, made extensive use of this plant that is, is fact, closely related to parsley. The fresh leaves are used as well as the dried fruits. Coriander is a stimulant, digestive, and carminative. In ancient times it was said to induce a state of euphoria and was added to wine to make it more intoxicating.

The herb is not universally popular, however. Some people consider its leaves to be foul-smelling. It is rarely used in French cuisine and is not used at all in Provençal cooking. On the other hand, it is so omnipresent in the cooking of other parts of the Mediterranean, such as Morocco, that it can be found almost year-round in the markets of Provence. Personally, I am rather fond of its slightly "exotic" taste and I often use it to flavor a vegetable soup—in the same way as I might use chervil—or to give more character to certain summer salads.

Sea-Bream Salad with Peaches

~

The planetary conjunction of July 8th 1983—I jotted down the date in my kitchen notebook—must have favored creativity because that was the day on which I invented this recipe that never fails to impress my friends when I serve it each summer.

PREPARATION. Squeeze the juice of seven lemons into a large bowl. Slice a few fillets of sea bream into thin diagonal slices about 1 inch (3 cm) thick. You should allow about 5 1/2 ounces (150 g) per person. Place the pieces of fish in the lemon juice to marinate. Cover with plastic wrap and chill for two hours.

Carefully peel two white peaches that are ripe but not overripe. These are July peaches. Slice them into quarters. Remove the outer skin from four or five shallots and cut them into thin slices. Pull the leaves from a small handful of coriander and do the same with a slightly smaller bunch of mint. Discard the stalks.

Just before serving, drain the fish, and arrange it in a bowl. Mix it with the quartered peaches. Add the herbs. Salt lightly, pepper generously, and sprinkle with a little olive oil.

This is a refreshing and elegant appetizer, perfect for the dog days of summer. It should be accompanied by a round white wine, such as one from the Domaine de Courtade at Porquerolles.

Coriander Butter

~

Coriander butter is a condiment, like mustard or ketchup, which I serve in summer with grilled meats or vegetables such as eggplant or zucchini. The recipe is basically the same as for a Maître d'Hôtel butter, but it needs much less butter and far more herbs.

PREPARATION. Remove the leaves from a large bunch of coriander and discard the stems. Peel two garlic cloves and remove the germ. Put the coriander, garlic, 1/4 cup (50 g) butter, and a little salt and pepper into a marble mortar or the bowl of a mixer, and reduce to a paste.

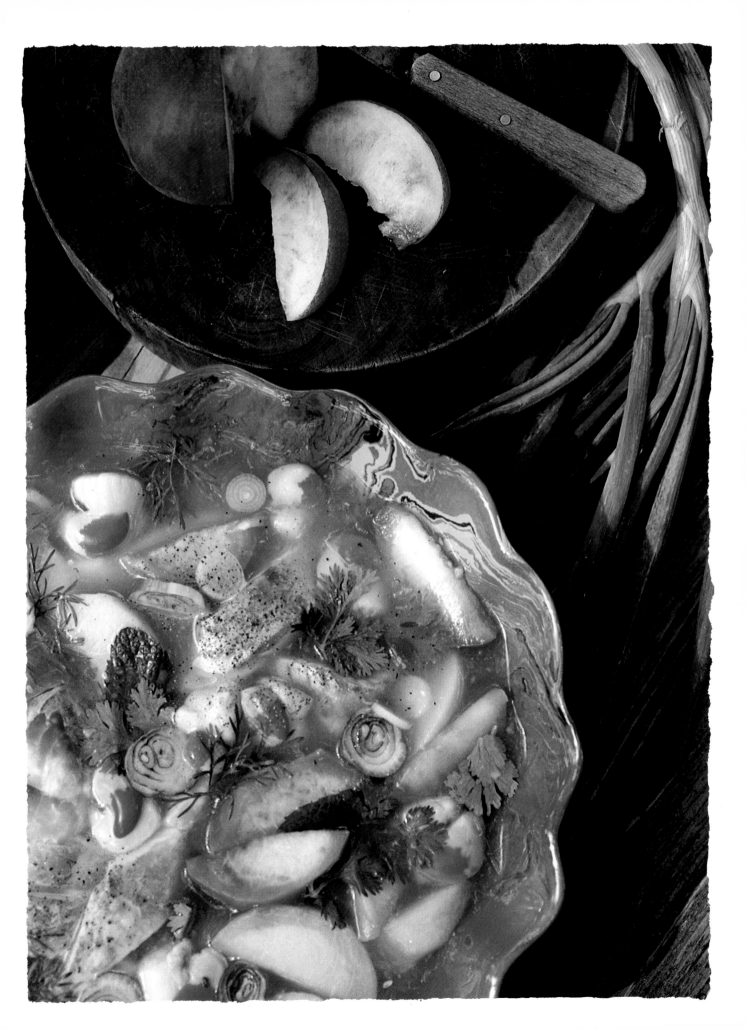

The paste should be dark green in color, the butter is merely there to bind the mixture. Put the coriander butter into a bowl, cover it with a sheet of plastic wrap, and refrigerate until ready to serve.

Tuscany Bread Salad

~

To make this hearty but exquisite salad, you will need ten or more slices of day-old bread, made from half all-purpose flour, half whole-wheat flour. Crumble the bread into a large bowl and sprinkle with cold water so that it is soggy. Then, squeeze the bread in your hands to extract as much water as possible. Discard the water and put the bread into a bowl. Add a small handful of coriander leaves, a few parsley leaves, and a few mint leaves, as well as a ripe, coarsely chopped tomato, a small, thinly sliced white onion, a chopped hard-boiled egg, salt, and freshly ground black pepper. Mix carefully, then refrigerate for at least for two hours.

Meanwhile, make a tomato vinaigrette by crushing a very ripe tomato with a fork. Add a tablespoon of wine vinegar, salt, and pepper. Finish with 1/3 cup (100 ml) of fruity olive oil and mix well. Just before serving, pour the vinaigrette into the

center of the bread salad. Garnish with a few black olives and a few coriander leaves and toss the salad lightly at table.

As with all salads, the acidity may spoil the flavor of the wine. So first take a large mouthful of bread to eliminate the acidity, then enjoy a generous rosé such as a Tavel from the Domaine de la Mordorée.

Tuna in Herb Packets

~

Skin a large piece of tuna about 2 inches (5–6 cm) thick and remove the central bone. Slice it into four to six steaks. Salt and pepper on both sides. Pull the leaves from a small bunch of coriander and discard the stalks. Trim, wash, and drain two nice round heads of lettuce, leaving the leaves whole. Wrap each tuna steak in coriander leaves, then in lettuce leaves, and arrange them in the top part of a couscous pot or a steamer. Bring two quarts (2 liters) of water to the boil and steam these herb packets of tuna for at least 20 minutes.

Personally, I do not like over-cooked tuna, I prefer it pink in the center. Serve very hot, sprinkled with lemon juice and a little olive oil, accompanied with a rice pilaf, for example.

Enjoy with a full-bodied, mellow wine such as a Saint-Péray, the great white wine of the Ardèche. If it comes from the cellars of Bernard Gripa or Alain Voge, it will be a wonderful discovery and will harmoniously prolong the pleasure of the tuna and herbs.

MINT

Mint is probably the best known and the most popular of all herbs. Mint pastilles, green mint syrups, mint tea, and even mint toothpaste flavoring have all made their contribution to this notoriety. Wild mint grows on the hillsides in abundance, distilling a delicate aroma when crushed underfoot, though today's hiker usually walks right by. There are several varieties of mint: peppermint, spearmint, watermint, and pennyroyal. All have long been picked for their tonic, stimulant, and antispasmodic properties, but today they are usually just seen as part of the scenery of the *garrigue*.

The cultivated mints are better known. Peppermint is much used in the production of menthol, but for cookery purposes, the most interesting is spearmint. It is very easy to grow in deep, fertile, cool soil. It propagates through the roots and can even spread like a weed unless you are careful. Plant two or three bunches of green mint in spring or fall. Water them a little and they will soon multiply and produce an abundant harvest every year.

John Malkovich's Turkish Pasta

~

To see the way he plays cruel, perverted, even monstrous characters on the screen with such immense talent, it is hard to believe what a generous, cultured, and delightful host he is, as well as being an inspired cook. As our neighbor, John treats us to a cosmopolitan and eclectic cuisine that borrows its accents from the same Orient that has always inspired Provence and that works so well with local flavors and colors. This is his recipe for Turkish-style pasta, which so superbly combines garlic, olive oil, and lamb with mint, lemons, and pine nuts.

PREPARATION. First wash two untreated lemons. Peel off the zest and slice it into narrow strips. In a large bowl, mix 2 cups (500 ml) of yogurt or clabbered milk with four tablespoons of a good, fruity olive oil. Add the lemon zest, the juice of two lemons, two finely chopped garlic cloves, a few grinds of pepper, and a large pinch of salt.

Have your butcher bone a shoulder of lamb and cut it into ten serving pieces. Heat some olive oil in a heavy-based pot and brown the meat in it over a high heat. Deglaze the pan with a half cup (125 ml) of water. Season with salt and pepper, then cover the pot and reduce the heat. Let it simmer for about 20 minutes. Meanwhile, in a large pot of boiling salted water, cook 1 pound (500 g) of large pasta such as *penne* or *orichiette*.

Now wash a large bunch of mint, dry it in a cloth, and remove the leaves. Then chop the meat fairly coarsely (it is not supposed to be ground). Return the meat to the pot to keep it warm.

When the pasta is cooked, act fast. Drain quickly and mix it with the yogurt, the chopped meat, whole mint leaves, and cup (100 g) pine nuts. Season to taste and serve this delicious, warm, fragrant salad immediately.

The most appropriate wine for this Oriental dish would be a Syrah with its berry aromas and full body, such as one from the Tain-l'Hermitage cellar or the more complex Côtes-de-Provence from the Domaine Richeaume.

Fresh Green Pea Soup

~

This is a recipe from the Nice hinterland. It dates right back to the days when domestic economy ensured that nothing went to waste. It not only uses the peas, therefore, but also the pods that are usually discarded. The result is perfect.

PREPARATION. Shell 2 1/4 pounds (1 kg) of garden peas and reserve them. Carefully wash the pods and soak them in water for about two hours. Drain, then cook them with a sliced onion in 1 quart (1 liter) of boiling water for about 20 minutes. When the pods are cooked, pour the contents of the pan into a food processor, then push it through a fine sieve to eliminate any tough pieces of pod.

Heat olive oil in a heavy-based pan. Gently fry a thinly sliced onion with a bunch of freshly picked mint leaves sliced into thin strips. Stir frequently so that the onion becomes transparent and golden, but do not let it brown. Add the shelled peas and a little water. Cover the pan. Simmer for about 20 minutes, perhaps less if the peas are very small.

Pour the pod purée over the peas, and season to taste with salt and pepper. Add a few drops of uncooked olive oil and serve very hot.

Minted Eggplant

~

Wash and dry 2 1/4 pounds (1 kg) of small eggplant. Trim the stem end and make a cross-shaped incision in it about 1/2 inch (1 cm) deep. Bring three quarts (3 liters) of salted water to the boil. Add the eggplant to it and cook for 15 minutes.

Meanwhile, in a large bowl, combine half a cup (125 ml) wine vinegar, three or four chopped garlic cloves, a large handful of chopped mint, a large pinch of salt, a sliced red chili pepper, a tablespoon of crushed peppercorns, and a few grinds of pepper. Let the garlic and mint infuse and the salt dissolve.

Drain the eggplant well and pull apart with your hands starting at the incision that you made. Then add one cup (250 ml) of olive oil to the vinegar mixture and beat this vinaigrette dressing. Arrange a layer of eggplant strips in a shallow bowl then cover them with the minted vinaigrette. Arrange another layer of strips on top, sprinkle with the vinaigrette and so on, until all the eggplant has been used. Pour the rest of the vinaigrette over the top layer. Add enough olive oil to ensure that the eggplant is covered with liquid. Cover the bowl with plastic wrap and refrigerate at least until the next day. It tastes best if left for 48 hours.

Serve as an appetizer with large slices of toasted whole-wheat bread or as an accompaniment to cold meat.

Savory Eggplant Mold
~

This traditional Provençal dish is called a *papeton*, surely dating from the days when the popes reigned in Avignon.

PREPARATION. Have the butcher bone a shoulder of lamb, then cut it into pieces about the size of an egg. Fry the pieces of lamb in olive oil in a Dutch oven or casserole with three sliced onions, a carrot sliced into rings, two chopped garlic cloves, salt and pepper. As soon as the meat starts to color, add one cup (250 ml) of broth. Cover the pot and reduce the heat. Simmer for one hour on very low heat, then remove from the heat and allow to cool.

Meanwhile, wash and wipe 3 1/3 pounds (1.5 kg) of eggplant. Trim the stems and use a kitchen knife to slit them lengthwise from the stem end. Bake whole for 20 minutes in a preheated hot (400°F/200°C) oven as you would for eggplant caviar. Remove the eggplant from the oven and scoop out the flesh with a spoon, taking care not to damage the skins, which should be reserved. Mash the eggplant flesh with three whole eggs, two teaspoons of sweet paprika, two tablespoons of chopped mint, a large pinch of marjoram leaves, salt, and pepper.

Grind the lamb finely and mix the ground meat with the eggplant. Carefully oil a mold and arrange the eggplant skins in it, purple side downward of course. Then fill the mold with the mixture. Bake the mold in a baking pan half-filled with warm water in a moderate (350°F/175°C) oven for 45 minutes. Unmold and serve hot with a generous helping of tomato sauce containing a little chili pepper.

To accompany this dish with its strong flavors, choose a Châteauneuf-du-Pape such as Vielle Vigne produced by Michel Tardieu and Dominique Laurent at Lourmarin. It will enchant you with its intense fruitiness and spicy notes.

Alain the Hairdresser's Peach Soup

~

Our friends in Isle-sur-la-Sorgue include Alain and Alain. So, to make things easier, we call them Alain the grocer and Alain the hairdresser. It is Alain the hairdresser who makes this wonderful peach soup.

Begin by reserving 20 of the best-looking leaves from a bunch of mint; they will be used to garnish the dish. Make an infusion of the rest, or at least as many as your teapot will hold, along with 15 sugar lumps. Fill the pot with boiling water and leave it to infuse for about 10 minutes.

before garnishing with the reserved mint leaves.

Meanwhile, peel 2 1/4 pounds (1 kg) of yellow peaches and slice them in a shallow serving bowl. Pour the hot infusion over the peaches through a strainer and wait until the liquid has cooled completely

Serve this soup with a well-chilled Beaumes-de-Venise Muscat, such as one from the Domaine de Durban with its fragrance of flowers and stewed peaches.

Minted eggplant (following double page).

LEMON BALM

My grandmother's medicine chest consisted of Carmelite balm water, baking soda, and Vichy lozenges. I remember that the balm water was kept in a little bottle with a black Bakelite screw-on top. It lived in the large drawer in the chest in her room and was brought out to cure almost anything, from little cuts and bruises to a major trauma, from trapped wind to constipation, including the vapors and colic. It was even taken with us on vacation, to try and relieve the horrible car sickness to which we always fell prey on long journeys, as soon as we left the freeway to take those interminable, winding side-roads beside the Gorge du Verdon or up the Montagne de Lure. I loved this remedy because it was administered in the form of a few drops on a lump of sugar, and it smelled and tasted good. And, if I remember rightly, it was also quite effective.

Not so long ago, balm or lemon balm was quite a common herb that grew beside houses, against walls and on embankments, amidst the nettles and other "weeds." It is a perennial, growing in clumps, with lots of pairs of bright green, oval, dentate leaves facing each on either side of the stem. Its special feature, however, is that it exudes a deliciously sweet lemon fragrance. Unfortunately, the upkeep of villages in modern times, the encroachment of paved roads, and the use of defoliants has caused lemon balm to become rarer. However, you will have no difficulty in finding it for sale in all good plant nurseries and garden centers. But be sure to plant it where it will be exposed to the sun, it hates the cold and damp.

Herbed Yogurt
~

I well remember the octagonal red Bakelite box in which my mother made delicious yogurt every evening. It contained eight white angular porcelain pots, plus a tiny pot in the center to hold the next day's starter. Then, the yogurt box disappeared in one of our moves and we started buying it at the grocery store. I also remember how a few years later, during a trip to the Middle East, I was so delighted to find large, glazed terra-cotta bowls, full to the brim with exquisite, thick, creamy yogurt. The size of these bowls matched my appetite far better than did the little porcelain pots. It was in Syria that I finally learned how to make yogurt myself, and here is the recipe.

PREPARATION. Combine 1 quart (1 liter) of fresh whole milk with 1 cup (125 g) full-cream milk powder and bring to a boil. Remove from the heat and leave to cool until the temperature reaches 100°F (45°C). Use a thermometer to test the temperature. When the correct heat is reached, pour 7 tablespoons (100 ml) of the warm milk into a cup and mix it with a commercial whole milk live yogurt. Pour the mixture into a glazed terra-cotta bowl. Cover with a plate, then wrap the bowl in several layers of thick cloth and do not touch it for six hours, or if you are making the yogurt in the evening, leave it until the following morning. Then unwrap and place in the refrigerator until you are ready to use it.

Serve this delicious yogurt as a dessert with liquid honey or stewed fruit, or make it into an herbed yogurt.

Wash and peel a large cucumber and grate it on a fine grater, as you would for carrots. Drain the grated cucumber in a sieve for a few minutes. Meanwhile, chop garden mint, lemon balm, and a few chives. Skin a couple of shallots and cut them into thin slices. Pour four ladles of yogurt into a large bowl and combine them with the grated cucumber, the chopped herbs, and sliced shallots. Season with salt and pepper and serve chilled as an appetizer.

Sea Bass with
Lemon Balm Butter

~

The delicate lemony fragrance of lemon balm is an excellent accompaniment to fish. I therefore suggest that you cook the sea bass simply in a package, accompanied by melted lemon balm butter and a pan of fresh spinach tossed in butter or oil. Of course, the spinach can be replaced by young poppy shoots, but if so, the poppies should first be blanched for a few minutes in salted boiling water and well drained before tossing them in butter or oil. If you can't find lemon balm, this recipe will taste just as good—though very different in personality—with a basil-flavored butter.

PREPARATION. First prepare the spinach. Wash and sort 3 1/3 pounds (1.5 kg) of spinach. Trim it and discard any discolored leaves. Drain well. Melt a lump of butter with a little olive oil in a large frying pan and lightly brown two thinly sliced white onions on low heat. When the onions are transparent, add the spinach gradually in handfuls as it wilts in the pan. When all the spinach has wilted, season it with salt and pepper. That's it!

While the spinach is cooking, gut a sea bass weighing about 3 1/3 pounds (1.5 kg).

Wash it in running water and wipe it dry, inside and out, with paper towels. Place a few branches of fresh lemon balm in the cavity. Lay the fish on a large sheet of aluminum foil and carefully fold the package to seal it. Bake it in a preheated hot (425°F/220°C) oven for no longer than 20 minutes.

Meanwhile, in a double boiler, melt 3/4 cup (200 g) butter. When the butter has melted, remove it from the heat, and add a pinch of salt, the juice of half a lemon, and a large handful of finely chopped lemon balm leaves. Return the mixture to the double boiler, off the heat, to keep it warm.

Remove the fish from the oven and let it rest inside its aluminum package for a few minutes before opening it. Remove the lemon balm branches inside the cavity before serving, accompanied by the spinach and lemon balm butter.

Serve with the elegant white wine produced by Allen Chevalier (Château Constantin-Chevalier), a good Côtes-du-Luberon with a pleasant aroma of white fruit that is typical of the appellation.

Lemon
Balm Brittle
~

Let us begin with the most difficult part, the brittle. This is a sort of praline that should be delicately lacy. To achieve this, I will let you in on one of the "cookery secrets" of my friend, the brilliant patissier, Pierre Hermé.

This is a very exacting recipe and you will need to buy a candy thermometer for the caramel, but if you like making patisserie and cooking sugar syrups you will soon find that it has been a useful purchase.

Take 1 1/2 cups (150 g) shelled almonds and blanch them in boiling water for a few moments so as to be able to remove their brown skins. Toast them lightly on a cookie sheet in the oven for 15 minutes. They should be slightly colored, at most reddish-brown, but not dark brown or they will be bitter. Place them between two large sheets of brown paper and crush them into tiny pieces with a rolling pin, enjoying the lovely odor they have at that moment. Do not crush them to powder, they should still be in small pieces.

In a large heavy-based saucepan, melt together 1/2 cup (125 g) butter, 2/3 cup (150 g) granulated sugar, 4 tablespoons glucose syrup (or 8 tablespoons light corn syrup), and 3 tablespoons of milk. My friend Pierre adds 2 tablespoons (15 g) cocoa powder, but this is not necessary for the recipe. Cook the liquid until it reaches 215°F (106°C), stirring gently with a spatula. Then incorporate the almonds while they are still hot. Spread this mixture as thinly as possible between two sheets of silicone release paper or nonstick baking paper, rolling it out with a rolling pin. Transfer the sheets to a cookie sheet and place in the freezer for 1 hour. Then remove the top sheet and bake the mixture in a preheated oven at 325°F (170°C) for 18 minutes. It is during the second cooking that the mixture shrinks and forms holes, looking like lacework. Remove it from the oven and break it into pieces of different sizes. Reserve them. That is how the brittle is made.

The rest is child's play. In a bowl, combine one pound (500 g) of goat's or sheep's Brousse cheese with the juice of a lemon, a little grated lemon zest, and 2/3 cup (100 g) of granulated sugar. Crush the mixture with a fork but do not beat it, the Brousse should be in crumbs. Use a fork to shape the cheese into a round cake and place it on a serving platter. Refrigerate it until the last moment. Just before serving, cover the whole surface of the cheese with

Sea bass with lemon balm butter (following double page).

small, freshly picked lemon balm leaves, or use mint if you cannot find lemon balm, and stick the pieces of brittle in it.

This handsome dessert deserves a Banyuls of good quality such as a Cellier des Templiers. Choose an old vintage, such as 1985 or 1988, or one that is *hors d'âge*, and wonder at its powerfully aromatic bouquet that ranges from preserved figs to coffee, and the explosion of flavors in the mouth which are reminiscent of truffles and leather, coffee and chocolate.

BAY LEAF

The bay leaf, faithful companion of parsley and thyme in a bouquet garni for stews, broth, and braised meats, is also known in French as "Apollo's laurel." Legend has it that Daphne, a chaste nymph who lived in the days of Mount Olympus, was unable to escape the assiduous attentions of the ardent Apollo. In order to save herself from him, she begged the gods to change her into a laurel bush and this was done immediately. But Apollo, who was bitterly unhappy at this transformation, made this evergreen tree his emblem in memory of his beloved. Henceforth, the priestesses of Apollo and the victors in the ancient Olympic Games dedicated to him were named "laureates," as were heroes and sages, and later emperors and graduates, all crowned with laurel wreaths, the symbol of glory—the glory of battle as much as of the intellect. The word "baccalauréat," the examination sat by French school-leavers, is also derived from the Latin *bacca lauri*, or "laurel berry."

The bay laurel should not be confused with the cherry laurel or common laurel which is toxic, nor with the very poisonous mountain laurel, which is native to North America.

The other French name for the bay laurel, apart from *laurier d'Apollon*, is *laurier sauce*, or sauce laurel, which leads us straight to the cooking pot.

Bay Tree
Twig Soup

~

This is a very old, even ancient, recipe, its origins lost in the mists of time. It is the ancestor of polenta and the Provençal cousin of Scots porridge. It is not really a recipe, more of a cooking method, a good way of making a soup "tasty."

PREPARATION. You will need a heavy-bottomed pan so that the soup does not stick and burn. Boil 2 quarts (2 liters) of water in it. Throw in three peeled and coarsely chopped onions, three unpeeled garlic cloves, one bay leaf, three sage leaves, and a handful of coarse salt. When the water boils in the pot, reduce the heat, and add 4 cups (500 g) of all-purpose flour mixed with just enough cold water to make a smooth batter, to prevent the formation of lumps. The flour could also be spelt flour, fine cornmeal, gram (chickpea) flour, or bean flour. You could add a ham hock or two pieces of leg of lamb, but this is not necessary.

The most important part is the laurel twig, from which the leaves have been removed, that is used for stirring the soup as it thickens. The soup is ready when the twig can stand up in it unaided.

Add a little olive oil and the soup is ready to warm a winter evening.

Onion *Tian*

~

Remove the outer skin from 2 1/4 pounds (1 kg) of white onions. Then blanch them in salted boiling water for about 30 minutes. Leave to drain in a sieve for at least one hour. Make a slit in each one with a sharp kitchen knife and insert a bay leaf.

Take a *tian*, a glazed pottery gratin dish, and pour a little olive oil into it. Fill it with the onions, packing them tightly against each other. Sprinkle with a little olive oil and pepper. Bake the *tian* in a preheated gentle oven (300°F/150°C) for 2 hours, basting it from time to time with the cooking juices. Serve hot as an accompaniment to a veal roast, for example.

The smoothness of this onion stew calls for a supple, seductive wine. These qualities can be found in the Marcel Juge Cornas, an elegant red with mild tannins and a floral nose, or in the Vielle Vigne Cornas, produced by Michel Tardieu and Dominique Laurent.

Stewed Jerusalem Artichokes

~

Although Jerusalem artichokes are delicious, they fell out of favor for a while because they reminded people of wartime austerity, and so recalled unhappy memories. My mother talked of them occasionally, but I never tasted them in my childhood.

They deserve to be rediscovered today for their delicate artichoke flavor and firm flesh. This old recipe comes from Haute-Provence and I am giving it here because bay leaf is the only herb it uses.

PREPARATION. Wash, peel, and slice 2 1/4 pounds (1 kg) of Jerusalem artichokes. Bring three quarts (3 liters) of lightly salted water, with a dash of vinegar, to a boil. Blanch the Jerusalem artichokes for about 10 minutes, then drain.

Add a little olive oil to a heavy-based pan and, over a low heat, cook 5 1/2 ounces (150 g) of diced salt pork, a sliced onion, a sliced leek, two crushed and peeled garlic cloves with the germ removed, two bay leaves, and a piece of dried orange zest. Cook until the mixture browns lightly, stirring from time to time, for about 15 minutes. Then add the Jerusalem artichokes, one cup (250 ml) tomato sauce, 1 1/4 cups (300 ml) warmed red wine, and the same quantity of warm water. When the liquid comes to a boil, cover the pot, and reduce the heat. Simmer for 30 minutes before removing the lid and continuing to cook for another 30 minutes so that the liquid evaporates. Serve hot as an appetizer.

With this strongly flavored dish, you will need a hearty, robust wine such as a Gigondas of good provenance. I am thinking of Les Hauts de Montmirail produced by Daniel Brusset, or those of the Domaine de Goubert, both of which are full-bodied and age well.

ANISEED

In Provence, aniseed-flavored pastis is mainly drunk at the local bistro, among men at the bar or on the terrace under the welcome shade of a plane tree. At home, anisette is served with water and ice cubes, accompanied by snacks such as olives, or small quiches filled with anchovy or olive paste. Ladies and children are most often served aniseed syrup. Homemade anisette and aniseed syrup are, like all the traditional drinks of Provence, jealously guarded family secrets for which unparalleled virtues are claimed; if one were to believe the women who make them, they are veritable elixirs of eternal youth. Aniseed syrup is not merely a delicious drink, it is also a great cure for hiccups. Just swallow a glass of cold water, containing two tablespoons of syrup, in one gulp without taking a breath! As for anisette, it contains all the stomachic, stimulant, and sedative properties of the herb.

But it is in Provençal patisserie that aniseed stands out. Honey cakes, the Christmas cake known *Gibassier,* see p. 112), a similar cake called *pompe à l'huile,* and many kinds of cookies (see p. 113) all are flavored with green aniseed.

My Grandmother Athalie's Anisette Liqueur

~

Macerate 2/3 cup (100 g) of crushed green aniseed with a pinch of ground coriander, another of ground cinnamon, two cloves, the zest of a dried orange peel, and a split vanilla bean in two quarts (2 liters) *eau-de-vie*. Leave for two weeks, then strain the liquid and add 2 quarts (2 liters) water in which 6 2/3 pounds (3 kg) of sugar have been dissolved. That is all there is to it.

Anisette is drunk neat as a liqueur or diluted with ice water as an aperitif.

Aniseed
Syrup

~

On the previous evening, bring 2 quarts (2 liters) water to the boil with 2/3 cup (100 g) green aniseed, a piece of licorice root and 1/8 teaspoon grated nutmeg. Then extinguish the heat and leave to infuse overnight.

Strain the liquid and add 4 1/2 pounds (2 kg) sugar. Return the liquid to the heat to allow the sugar to melt but remove it from the heat as soon as it comes to a boil. Leave to cool then put in bottles. Aniseed syrup is drunk heavily diluted with ice-cold water.

Christmas
Star Cake

~

This Christmas Star Cake or *Gibassier* is one of the traditional thirteen desserts served in Provence at supper on Christmas Eve after Midnight Mass, along with almonds, walnuts, nougat, grapes, dates, and figs.

PREPARATION. Sift 2 1/4 pounds (1 kg) flour into a bowl. Add 1 1/4 cups (300 g) sugar, a pinch of salt, 3/4 cup (200 ml) olive oil, and 2 tablespoons (25 g) fresh yeast, dissolved in 1 cup (250 ml) warm orange-flower water. Add 1/3 cup (125 g) diced candied orange peel and 3 teaspoons green aniseed. Stir, then knead the mixture as if you were making bread. This

calls for muscle power, since the longer the dough is kneaded the better the finished cake will be. Roll the dough into a ball, cover it with a damp cloth, and leave it to rise in a warm room for about two hours.

Divide the dough into four portions. Flatten each one with a rolling pin to make four circles about the thickness of a finger. Use a sharp knife to make five cuts in a star shape, starting from the center of each circle. This is to symbolize the star seen by shepherds. Arrange each of the circles on an oiled and floured cookie sheet and bake in a preheated hot (425°F/220°C) oven for about 30 minutes.

Aniseed Cookies

~

Make a batter using 2 cups (250 g) all-purpose flour, 3/4 cup (175 g) granulated sugar, 1/4 cup (50 g) softened butter, 2 tablespoons (15 g) green aniseed and 2 tablespoons orange-flower water. Knead it just enough for it to stick together, but no longer. Roll it into a ball, wrap in plastic wrap and leave to rest in a cold place for 1 hour.

Roll out the dough with a rolling pin until it is about 1/4 in (8 mm) thick. Use a glass to cut out circles and place them on a greased and floured cookie sheet. Bake the cookies in a preheated gentle oven (325°F/160°C) for no longer than 15 minutes. Traditionally, aniseed cookies should not brown. Leave them to cool on a cake rack. If you do not intend to eat them immediately, which would surprise me, store them in an airtight tin.

ARUGULA

Arugula flower.

Another wild salad green, arugula, also called rocket salad, is strongly flavored and grows in colonies on fallow land. It has long been cultivated in the Nice region and is a key ingredient of the green salad known as Mesclun (see recipe on p. 115). An annual with a pointed stem, it bears lyre-shaped leaves and white or yellow flowers streaked with violet.

Aphrodisiac properties have been attributed to arugula since Antiquity. In the Middle Ages, it was used to prepare an elixir, the Electuary of Satyrio, whose purpose was to "rehabilitate organs exhausted by debauchery or worn out with old age." So powerful were the properties attributed to this herb that its cultivation in monastery gardens was forbidden! Whatever the case, most books on herbs advise using arugula in moderation.

The difference between wild and cultivated arugula is much greater than the difference in other herbs. Wild rocket is very strong, rather peppery, acrid, and strongly scented. It is used as an aromatic to flavor cream cheese, salad, or potatoes. The milder, cultivated variety has a flavor that resembles hazelnuts. On its own, it makes a delicious salad.

Mesclun Nice-Style

~

The green salad that is a specialty of Nice is called Mesclun, a word derived from the local word *mescla* which means "mixture." For more than a hundred years, the truck farmers of Nice and the Var Valley have made this salad their specialty. It is very probable that they merely appropriated the popular custom of making salads from a mixture of wild greens. Any Provençal salad greens can be included in this Mesclun—dandelion, arugula, purslane, lamb's lettuce, romaine lettuce, escarole, watercress, parsley, chervil, or anise. Mesclun is traditionally green, and only recently have red and purple leaves been added, including Rougette de Montpellier, a red-and-green-leafed lettuce.

Since Mesclun is a strongly flavored salad, the only dressing it needs is a thin stream of olive oil, a little lemon juice, and a pinch of salt.

Fresh Goat's Cheese with Wild Arugula

~

The little rounds of fresh goat's cheese that can be found throughout Provence are very suitable for mixing with chopped herbs. Here are two recipes: one using wild arugula, to make a simple, fresh-tasting appetizer, the other, more spectacular, contains a wider variety of herbs, thus requiring slightly more preparation.

PREPARATION. You will need about 20 arugula leaves, preferably wild ones, freshly picked from the top of the plant where the shoots are more tender. Chop them finely and mix with four small fresh goat's cheeses, salt, and pepper. Place in a bowl and cover with plastic wrap; refrigerate 1 hour.

Serve with large slices of warm, toasted whole-wheat bread, sprinkled with a little Nyons olive oil, and drink a white Saint-Joseph '94 produced by Bernard Gripa, with its delicate fragrances of white flowers and smoothness in the mouth.

Fresh Goat's Cheeses
with Garden Herbs

~

If you are lucky enough to live in Isle-sur-la-Sorgue, as I do, this recipe is not for you. You can buy these attractive herbed cheeses in the market, and frankly, you could do no better yourself. Otherwise, read on.

PREPARATION. Begin by buying at least a pound (500 g) of good, fresh goat's cheese, as well as all the fresh herbs you can find, such as arugula, chives, mint, coriander, parsley, basil, tarragon, thyme in flower, and wild thyme. You will also need some young garlic, salt, and pepper. It is extremely important that the herbs are fresh and tender, and they must not be dried, it is a matter of texture. That is why

rosemary, for example, is unsuitable: the leaves are much too tough to blend well with the soft goat's cheese.

Divide the goat's cheese into as many patties as there are different types of herb, plus an extra one for the garlic. Then choose the most attractive coriander and parsley leaves, the prettiest thyme flowers, a few perfect chives, and three short, juicy sprigs of wild thyme and mint, all of which should be reserved for the decoration. Carefully sort the herbs, discarding any tough coriander, parsley, and tarragon stems, and any faded or damaged leaves. Then chop each herb separately, as finely as possible. Do the same with the garlic clove. Mix a little cheese into each pile of chopped herbs, in the proportion of one tablespoon of cheese to one teaspoon of herb, and perhaps a little less for the garlic. Then you can add a little salt and a few grinds of pepper, but that is not altogether necessary.

Now reshape each cheese into a little patty, decorating it with an attractive leaf or an herb flower to both flavor and identify it. I prefer to serve these delicious cheeses as an appetizer, with crusty, toasted whole-wheat bread and a flask of olive oil on the table.

Fresh goat's cheeses with wild arugula.

A white wine from the lovely estate of the Domaine de la Verrerie which is very fruity, round in the mouth, well-balanced, and with notes of honey would be a pleasant accompaniment to these cheeses.

Pizza
of the Redeemer
~

This recipe is a delightful travel souvenir. On the island of La Giudecca, in the Venice lagoon, facing the Zattere Quay, stands the handsome Palladian Church of the Redeemer (Il Redentore). La Giudecca is a very special part of Venice, in that it still retains the slow pace of village life, so different from the bustle of the city. Few tourists venture this far, except for a few fans of the architect Palladio, and residents at the youth hostel on the quay; both fall into the rare category of bearable tourists. The Trattoria de' Redentore is right next to the church. I have often lunched and dined there, taking advantage of the magnificent view that it offers of Venice, San Giorgio, and St. Mark's Square, and enjoying the simple Italian food. One of my favorite dishes is the pizza, served piping hot, smothered with tomatoes and mozzarella, and sprinkled with a thick layer of fresh, raw *ruccola*, which is none other than our arugula.

PREPARATION. Make a pizza as in the recipe on p. 121, arranging ten slices of mozzarella over the tomato. Sprinkle with a thin stream of olive oil. Bake for 15 minutes in a preheated hot (450°F/230°C) oven. As soon as you remove the pizza from the oven, sprinkle it all over with 2 1/2 cups (300 g) fresh, cultivated, washed and chopped arugula.

Serve immediately with a fruity, lively Côtes-du-Luberon rosé from the Domaine de la Citadelle.

LAMB'S LETTUCE

In English, lamb's lettuce is also called corn salad and in most parts of France it is known as *mâche*, but in Provence, it goes by the name *doucette*, which means "mild." It is certainly the commonest of the wild greens of Provence, growing everywhere from fields to holes in the walls. It is found in every garden and is sold in markets throughout the winter, since it is so easy to cultivate. As its botanical name, *Valerianiella olitoria*, indicates, lamb's lettuce belongs to the valerian family, though it does not possess the remarkable anti-spasmodic properties of valerian. It is simply a delicious salad green, tender and mild as its Provençal name implies.

Lamb's Lettuce Salad with Onions
~

Peel three or four onions and slice them thinly. Pour a little olive oil into a frying pan and cook the onions over a very low heat. Season with salt and pepper. The onions should be allowed to cook very gently but not to brown, or the flavor will be quite different.

Sort, wash, and drain the lamb's lettuce and arrange it in a salad bowl. When you are ready to serve the salad, sprinkle the cooked onions over it and mix well, then salt and pepper to taste. No need for any additional dressing. Serve alone as an appetizer, it is quite enough on its own.

OREGANO AND MARJORAM

Oregano and marjoram are often confused and sometimes one is sold as the other. In fact, the two herbs are closely related and are used very similarly as flavorings since they taste so much alike. Marjoram, also known as sweet marjoram, reached France via India, Arabia, and Egypt along the spice route of the Levant Ladder, and does not grow wild in Provence. One can imagine that among all the valuable merchandise unloaded on the Quai Saint-Jean in the port of Marseilles, among the bales of cotton, the sacks of cinnamon, the boxes of saffron, indigo, and coffee, the rolls of printed cotton fabrics from India and the rich silks from Damascus, there were a few sacks of marjoram. Oregano, on the other hand, is a wild plant that is very common in this part of the world. It grows in the meadows as well as on the dryer hillsides. Oregano is a perennial whose stems are sometimes tinted red; the leaves are gray-green, oval, and velvety, the flowers pink or mauve, growing in little bunches at the tops of the stems.

Like the other aromatic labiates, oregano has numerous medicinal properties that make it a valuable plant for treating loss of appetite, troublesome digestion, and intestinal fermentation. It was once used to alleviate childhood whooping cough and violent coughing fits in old people. Marjoram, like oregano, is strongly flavored and is thus much used in cooking, but it is best known as a flavoring for pizza, which has given it the nickname of "pizza herb."

Grated Carrots with Marjoram
~

Yes, this is a recipe for simple grated carrots, so familiar that it is rarely included in a cookbook. But fresh marjoram transforms this salad. Very little is needed, so strong is the flavor of the herb.

PREPARATION. Choose nice young carrots straight from the garden, freshly picked, washed, and dried. If they are really young and fresh, it would be a pity to peel them, so just scrape them lightly. Grate and mix them with a finely chopped garlic clove, the juice of a lemon, a good sprinkling of olive oil, salt, freshly ground pepper, and a pinch of fresh marjoram leaves. Mix well and serve immediately.

Pierre and Paul's Pizzas

~

Paul is my eldest son, Pierre-Grégoire is his friend, and both of them are the kings of pizza. What began in Naples as a savory tart has conquered the world in its various forms that range from the inedible to the utterly delicious. In Provence, in the late afternoon, at around five o'clock, "pizza trucks" roll into all the village squares. These are actually large vans, usually painted white and decorated with red lettering, with a wide flap on the side that opens out as a counter. Once the oven has been heated, it produces a delicious combination of odors of wood smoke, grilled cheese, and marjoram.

At home, we have rarely needed to avail ourselves of the services of the pizza-sellers for the past few years, ever since Paul began producing these pizzas. Here are all the secrets.

PREPARATION. You will need at least four hours to make the pizza because the leaven and then the bread dough need to rise. Begin by preparing a leaven by mixing 2 1/2 tablespoons (40 g) of fresh yeast with 4 tablespoons (50 ml) warm water. In a bowl, mix 4 tablespoons (60 g) of all-purpose flour with the dissolved yeast until you have a smooth dough. Work the dough into a ball, sprinkle it with a little sifted flour, and cut a cross in it with a knife. Cover it with a cloth and leave to rest for an hour at a temperature of 68°F (20°C).

Then add 4 cups (500 g) all-purpose flour and 5 tablespoons olive oil. A mild Nyons olive oil is perfect for the purpose. Add another 1/3 cup (100 ml) of water and work the dough vigorously for as long as possible, aerating it so that it becomes completely smooth. Shape it into a ball again and cover it with a cloth. Leave it to rest for two hours this time, again at a temperature of 68°F (20°C).

Divide the dough into two equal parts. Roll out the portions with a rolling pin into circles about 1/2 inch (1 cm) thick. Before doing so, you should have cooked five or six large, ripe, coarsely chopped tomatoes in a frying pan with a little salt and pepper, over a very low heat, for 45 minutes. Strain this sauce through a vegetable mill or sieve and let it cool completely before use. Then spread a ladle of the sauce over each circle of dough, leaving a border of about 3/4 inch (1.5 cm) around the edge.

Clean 15 salt anchovy fillets, and rinse them in running water. Dry them on paper towels and arrange them over the first pizza, adding a few black olives. Sprinkle with a good tablespoon of dried marjoram leaves (fresh marjoram is too strong for pizza). Sprinkle with a little olive oil and that's all there is to it. This is Pierre's favorite pizza.

After you have spread the tomato sauce over the second pizza, cover it with a thick layer of grated Gruyère cheese. Finish as for the anchovy pizza with a few black olives, marjoram, and a sprinkling of olive oil. This is Paul's favorite pizza.

They should now be baked in a really hot preheated oven (450°F/230°C) for no more than 15 minutes; serve them piping hot, accompanied by a flask of olive oil in which about thirty "bird's-eye" chili peppers and a couple of garlic cloves have been macerated for three weeks. Serve with a well-chilled bottle of Provençal rosé.

Anchovy pizza and cheese pizza are the simplest and most classic of pizzas. They are also the best, in my opinion, but of course you can have fun creating pizzas with artichokes, or onions, or squid, following the same method.

Oregano Butter

~

I am very fond of this oregano butter served well chilled to accompany broiled and grilled foods. It is very easy to make. The butter must be soft enough to be able to work it, but not overly so. Using a marble mortar and a wooden pestle or in the bowl of a mixer, crush a handful of fresh oregano leaves with a teaspoon of coarse salt. Then cut the butter into small pieces and add it, finishing with the juice of a lemon. Work it well until smooth then place it immediately in a little pot in the refrigerator where it should chill until just before being served with, for example, grilled or broiled lamb cutlets or slices of grilled zucchini, cooked over the embers.

You can make herb butter with any fresh, tender herbs such as tarragon and coriander, parsley, or sage, but I advise you to avoid dried herbs, or those that are too tough and woody, such as thyme and rosemary, for obvious reasons of texture.

SPINACH AND CHARD

I am well aware that spinach and chard are not herbs of Provence in the true sense of the word, but they are the basis for so many cooked greens that are popular from here right into northern Italy. They will enable you to create some of the recipes in this book, even if you cannot find fresh poppy shoots, purslane, or wild leeks. To this extent, they are so much a part of the traditional cuisine of Provence that they deserve a chapter all to themselves.

Chard Omelet
~

This omelet, with its cousin the tomato omelet, is traditionally eaten at picnics and by hunting parties, because it tastes even better cold and does not suffer from being made on the previous day. It is made with chard or spinach leaves, or any herbs that are at hand, a few wild leeks, poppy shoots, and nettles, a little arugula and lamb's lettuce, but not dandelion or chicory as these herbs are too bitter for an omelet.

On the other hand, you can easily add a few radish and turnip leaves. Although such a mixture of flavors is always interesting, if it is made with mere spinach and the green parts of chard leaves, the result is guaranteed to be good.

PREPARATION. Sort, wash, and drain chard leaves. Carefully detach the green parts of the leaves from around the stems and the white ribs. This is easy and quick to do. Reserve the white ribs for a gratin. Peel and slice an onion and cook it in olive oil in a large omelet or sauté pan over a low heat. When it is translucent, add the coarsely chopped chard leaves. Do not worry if it looks as though there are too many to fit in the frying pan, they will reduce considerably over the heat.

Sprinkle with a little salt and plenty of pepper. Let them reduce with the onion over a low heat, stirring from time to time until they are completely wilted and soft. Set aside.

Break about ten fresh eggs into a bowl, salt and pepper, then beat them with a fork to mix well, though take care not to overdo it. Add the herbs and mix again.

You now have a choice. If you are sure of your omelet pan, after re-heating it for a few seconds, you can pour the egg mixture back into it, despite the risk that it will stick, or you can wash and carefully dry the pan before putting it back on the fire with a little olive oil. The omelet should cook gently; stir it from time to time with a wooden spoon. When it is cooked on one side, pour it into an omelet-

turner or a large lid, then cook the other side. This delicious omelet can be eaten hot, warm, or cold.

It is difficult to recommend a wine to drink with an omelet but you might enjoy a subtle elegant rosé, such as the Cuvée Pétale de Rose of the Château de Barbeyrolles at Gassin.

Giorgio and Irène's
Risotto Verde
~

In a fanciful world in which elegance, humor, taste, and high culture mix, my friends Giorgio and Irène reign supreme. Their house stands on the banks of the Rhône, in a land of wild bulrushes and basketry, transformed for our pleasure into a baroque poem, a mixture of nomadic tent and Florentine palazzo. When we visit them, they sometimes serve this surprising green rice *al dente*.

Begin by washing and sorting 2 1/4 pounds (1 kg) of spinach, then blanch it in salted, boiling water for just four or five minutes, no longer. Drain well and leave it to cool before chopping it finely. Meanwhile prepare 1 quart (1 liter) broth: homemade chicken or beef broth would be perfect, but if that is not possible, use a stock cube. At the last moment, that is to

say, 25 minutes before serving the dish, heat olive oil in a frying pan and lightly brown three thinly sliced onions. Keep the heat very low because the onions should barely color and do not let them darken, or the flavor will be spoiled. To make this dish you could also use a heatproof glazed terra-cotta pot, so you can serve the risotto straight from the dish. When the onions are translucent, add one cup (250 g) short-grained Camargue rice per person. Increase the heat slightly and lightly brown the rice and onions together, stirring constantly with a wooden spoon, just long enough to sing a song. This is how Giorgio gave me the recipe, and this translates into the three minutes needed for the rice to become translucent. Add a cup (250 ml) of good dry white wine, the same wine that you will be serving with the dish, and allow it to be absorbed by the rice, stirring constantly. (This is a very stirring story.) Then cover the rice with hot broth, reduce the heat, and continue to stir for a good ten minutes. Add more broth whenever necessary to keep the mixture nice and moist. Then add the spinach and continue to cook for two minutes. By now, the rice should be *al dente*, that is to say still slightly firm to the bite. Remove it from the heat, because the rice will continue to cook in the pot and it will be perfect when you serve it in a few minutes. Once off the fire, stir in a bowl of grated Parmesan which should melt and bind the risotto.

Serve immediately, accompanied by a dry white wine with fragrance and roundness such as the white wines from the Domaine de la Citadelle at Ménerbes. The grape variety could be any one of Chardonnay, Viognier, or a Roussane-Marsane mixture; all are suitable for this brightly colored, delicately flavored rice dish.

Herb Flan

~

All sorts of garden herbs and greens are to be found in this flan. You need a few spinach leaves, a leek, a small lettuce, a few radish and turnip greens, and a few small fresh nettle leaves, to make a total weight of 1 pound (500 g) of herbs, which should be carefully picked over and washed, then coarsely chopped.

Slice the leek into 3-inch (7–8 cm) lengths, then slice these lengthwise into little strips. Bring 3 quarts (3 liters) of salted water to a boil and add the leeks as well as a small, thinly sliced onion. Cook for three minutes before adding the rest of the herbs. Cook for another four minutes, then carefully drain. As much water as possible should be extracted before mixing the herbs with four beaten eggs, salt and pepper, and 2 tablespoons of olive oil. Add 1/8 teaspoon of grated nutmeg and 2 tablespoons of finely chopped chives. Mix well before pouring this preparation into a buttered mold. Bake the herb flan in the oven, in a bain-marie, at 370°F/180°C, for at least 30 minutes. Leave it to cool and serve with a tomato sauce, slightly seasoned with Cayenne pepper.

Grilled Polenta
with Wild Herbs

~

In the traditional peasant cooking of the Nice hinterland and deep in the valleys of the upper Var, polenta was the staple daily dish. Depending on the days or the villages in question, it was accompanied by a walnut sauce or a little cheese, mushrooms, an anchovy sauce, or an herb sauce. And this last is the recipe that follows, though it is enriched with milk and herbs which were certainly not included in the classic version but which, I assure you, do nothing to spoil it.

In a large, deep pot, boil 2 cups (500 ml) whole milk with 2 cups (500 ml) water. Salt and pepper the liquid when it comes to a boil and sprinkle it with 1 3/4 cups (400 g) yellow cornmeal. I prefer a medium ground cornmeal, finely ground cornmeal makes the texture of the polenta too soft.

Bring the liquid back to the boil, stirring constantly with a wooden spoon. Remove it from the heat after a few minutes. Add 3 tablespoons of olive oil from the Nice district, 4 tablespoons (50 g) grated cheese, and 2 egg yolks. Mix well before spreading it in a gratin dish and leaving the polenta to cool completely. It will take the form of a compact block that you can cut with a knife into squares or triangles. There are then two ways of continuing. You can arrange the pieces without overlapping them in a gratin dish and sprinkle them with grated Gruyère and olive oil, then bake them in a preheated, very hot (450°F/230°C) oven. Or you can arrange the pieces of polenta on a grill and cook them over the embers turning them after 3–4 minutes. Whichever way you choose, serve them hot, accompanied by an herb and anchovy sauce.

What follows is almost a stew rather than a sauce. Any type of garden herb, sorted, washed, and trimmed, such as spinach or the green parts of chard, wild or cultivated leeks, nettle leaves, turnip and radish tops, lettuce or escarole, a little arugula, a little purslane, and a few parsley and mint leaves can be used. Any mixture of these herbs is fine. Cook them in a deep pot in a little olive oil, uncovered and on a fairly high heat, stirring constantly with a wooden spoon. The herbs will produce liquid at first. When it has evaporated, use the wooden spoon to make a little well in the center of the herbs in the pot. In this well, place seven or eight salt anchovy fillets that have been cleaned, washed in running water, and dried with paper towels. Reduce the heat to a minimum, and wait for a few moments until the anchovies have melted before mixing well and serving this herb-and-anchovy sauce.

Do not season it with salt or pepper, the anchovies are there to add saltiness, and a rosé wine from the Domaine de la Bernarde at Le Luc is sufficiently rich and concentrated to make a harmonious accompaniment to this dish.

GRAPE LEAVES
AND FIG LEAVES

Banon is a delightful village in Haute-Provence that is famous for the goat's cheese that bears its name. It is a wonderful creamy, supple cheese with a thin, white rind. To preserve and age it, the cheese is soaked in *eau-de-vie*, then wrapped in brown chestnut leaves that are tied in a package with a piece of raffia. It is then left for two weeks, after which it is a delight to untie the package, remove the leaves, and discover this delicious cheese that has fully benefited from the tannin-rich chestnut leaves that enclosed it. At one time, Banon was wrapped in vine leaves, and I do not know why the practice changed.

The practice of preserving or cooking food in leaves is common to many lands around the world. The Chinese steam delicious dim sum, little sticky rice patties containing meat and spices, rolled in lotus leaves. In Indonesia, rice is cooked in banana leaves, and the native Americans of New Mexico stuff corn stalks with cornmeal to make tamales. The stuffed grape leaves of Greece are famous and the women of Corsica use chestnut leaves in which to wrap the wonderful dessert of fragrant, lemon-flavored Brocciu cheese called *fiadone*. In all these examples, the leaves not only wrap and decorate the dish, but their tannin and fragrance pleasantly alter its taste and smell.

When you are out walking in Provence, gathering your stocks of thyme and fennel, salad herbs from the fields and wild leeks, do not forget to add a few tender, fresh grape leaves to the basket, as well as a few fig leaves. You can then try these three recipes.

Lamb Morsels in Grape Leaves

~

I am no longer sure of the origin of this recipe, it may be from Syria or Turkey. At any event, it is perfect for summer buffets and I often serve it to friends. Stuffed grape leaves are used in many cuisines around the Mediterranean, even as far away as Armenia, where they are stuffed with rice, raisins, and pine nuts, flavored with anise. On the island of Cyprus, the rice stuffing is mixed with ground veal and lamb, and flavored with fresh mint. But our recipe contains no rice at all, simply delicious little cubes of lamb.

PREPARATION. Choose about forty thin, tender grape leaves of average size. Wash them carefully and trim away the stems. Then blanch in boiling water for no longer than three minutes to make them pliable. Drain them.

Have your butcher bone two shoulders of lamb. Cut this meat into cubes and stuff each grape leaf with a piece of meat. Salt and pepper the meat before folding up the packet. Arrange the packets in a deep pot, interspersing them occasionally with a peeled garlic clove. Allow for a total of 15 garlic cloves. Use a thin, sharp-bladed knife to peel the zest from three or four untreated lemons. Slice the zests into small pieces and insert them among the grape-leaf packages. Add the juice of the lemons. Sprinkle with salt and with 3 tablespoons (50 g) butter cut into shavings. Place a large plate over the grape leaves and place a stone on the plate to keep the grape leaves in place during cooking. Completely cover with water, because you will need two cups (500 ml) broth for the sauce. Bring to the boil, then reduce the heat and simmer for 90 minutes. Drain the packets carefully.

There will be plenty of time, toward the end of the cooking, to prepare the lemon sauce. In a heavy-bottomed pan over low heat, melt 3 tablespoons (50 g) butter and mix 2 tablespoons flour into it. Simmer for 2 minutes but do not let the roux brown. Then, whisking constantly with a sauce whisk, pour in two cups (500 ml) of the cooking liquid, all at once. Whisk well to prevent the formation of lumps and stir constantly until the sauce thickens and bubbles. In a bowl, beat two egg yolks with the juice of half a lemon and add the hot sauce gradually, whisking constantly. Stir the sauce over a low heat and simmer for another two minutes, stirring gently. This dish can be served cold or hot with the vine leaves on a serving platter and the lemon sauce in a sauceboat.

To go with this strongly flavored dish you will need a robust wine, such as a Cornas by Auguste Clape, which is remarkably flavored, with very delicate tannins.

Corsican *Fiadone*
~

Use a fork to crush one pound (500 g) of fresh ewe's milk Corsican Brocciu or a similar Brousse cheese. Add 2/3 cup (150 g) sugar, three whole eggs one after the other, and finally the juice and grated zest of an untreated lemon. Take a dozen chestnut or grape leaves, wash them, remove the stems, and blanch them by throwing them into boiling water and leaving them for three minutes. Dry with paper towels, then place a little pile of cheese in the center of each leaf. Close the packet and turn it over so it lies seam downward in a gratin dish. Cook the *fiadone* for 25 minutes in a preheated hot (400°F/200°C) oven.

Leave to cool completely before serving with a nice, lively white wine from the Corsican Cape such as Clos-Nicrosi or a dessert wine from the same estate, a fruity, well-balanced Muscatellu made from the tiny Muscatel grapes.

Pierre Hermé's Fruit Wrapped in Fig Leaves

~

My friend Pierre Hermé, the famous and brilliant patissier, once gave me this recipe and I have used it several times every summer to the great delight of my family and friends. Thanks again, Pierre!

This time, go into the garden and pick some nice young fig leaves that are not too large. At the same time, pick a dozen ripe figs and a dozen superb apricots. Cut the fruit in half, remove the apricot pits, and place a teaspoon of sugar and a sprinkling of lemon juice in each piece of fruit. Close and wrap each piece in a fig-leaf packet. Arrange them carefully in a gratin dish.

Bake for about 20 minutes in a preheated hot (400°F/200°C) oven and serve the packets immediately accompanied by a delicious vanilla ice cream. The fragrance of the fig leaves will give the fruit an incomparable flavor.

For the wine, why not stay in Corsica, more specifically in Patrimonio, and accompany this subtle dessert with a delicious Muscat produced by Antoine Arena, with its bouquet of exotic fruits, that is rich but which has a pleasant freshness that will delight you.

A PERFECT WINE CELLAR

This list features wines from different regions of France that provide the ideal accompaniment for Provençal dishes. (The dialing code for France is 33. Drop the initial 0 of the number).

RHÔNE VALLEY

Côtes-du-Rhône

Domaine de Gramenon
    26770 Montbrison
    tel. : 04.75.53.57.08
Corinne Couturier
    La Font d'Estevenas
    84290 Cairanne
    tel. : 04.90.30.70.05
Domaine Marcel-Richaud
    Route de Rasteau
    84290 Cairanne
    tel. : 04.90.30.85.25
Domaine de l'Oratoire Saint-Martin
    Route de Saint-Roman
    84290 Cairanne
    tel. : 04.90.30.82.07
Domaine de la Soumade
    Route d'Orange
    84110 Rasteau
    tel. : 04.90.46.11.26

Crozes-Hermitage

Domaine Pochon
    Curson - 26600 Tain-l'Hermitage
    tel. : 04.75.07.34.60
Domaine Alain-Graillot
    Les Chênes Verts
    26600 Pont-de-l'Isère
    tel. : 04.75.84.67.52

Tavel

Domaine de la Mordorée
    30126 Tavel
    tel. : 04.66.50.00.75
Château d'Aqueria
    30126 Tavel
    tel. :04.66.50.04.56

Châteauneuf-du-Pape

Château de Beaucastel
    84350 Courthézon
    tel. : 04.90.70.41.00
Château de la Nerthe
    84230 Châteauneuf-du-Pape
    tel. : 04.90.83.70.11

Gigondas

Domaine du Cayron
    84190 Gigondas
    tel. : 04.90.65.87.46
Domaine Brusset
    84290 Cairanne
    tel. : 04.90.70.91.60
Domaine Les Goubert
    84190 Gigondas
    tel. : 04.90.65.86.38

Vacqueyras

Domaine des Amouriers
    84260 Sarrians
    tel. : 04.90.65.83.22
Domaine Le Sang des Cailloux
    84260 Sarrians
    tel. : 04.90.65.88.64

Hermitage

Chapoutier
    26600 Tain-l'Hermitage
    tel. : 04.75.08.28.65
Domaine J.-L. Chave
    07300 Mauves
    tel. : 04.75.08.24.63

Saint-Joseph et Saint-Péray

Domaine Bernard-Gripa
    07300 Mauves
    tel. : 04.75.08.14.96

Cornas

Domaine Auguste-Clape
    07130 Cornas
    tel. : 04.75.40.33.64

Saint-Péray

Alain Voge
    07130 Cornas
    tel. : 04.75.40.32.04

• Highly recommended:
Michel Tardieu et
Dominique Laurent
    84360 Lauris
    tel. : 04.90.08.32.07
Wines produced in the cellars of the Château de Lourmarin, made solely from old vines with a low yield. Here you will find excellent Côtes-du-Rhône, Cornas, Crozes-Hermitage, Vacqueyras, Hermitage, Châteauneuf-du-Pape and Côte-Rôtie.

PROVENCE

Côtes-du-Luberon and Côtes-du-Ventoux

Domaine de la Citadelle
    84560 Ménerbes
    tel. : 04.90.72.41.58
Château Constantin-Chevalier
    84160 Lourmarin
    tel. : 04.90.68.38.99
Domaine de la Verrerie
    84360 Puget-sur-Durance
    tel. : 04.90.08.26.64

Costières-de-Nîmes

Château Mourgues du Grès
    30300 Beaucaire
    tel. : 04.66.59.46.10

Côtes-de-Provence

Domaine Richeaume
    13114 Puyloubier
    tel. : 04.42.66.31.27
Domaine de la Bernarde
    83340 Le Luc
    tel. : 04.94.60.71.31

Château Réal Martin
  83143 Le Val
  tel. : 04.94.86.40.90
Domaine de la Courtade
  Porquerolles
  83400 Hyères
  tel. : 04.94.58.31.44
Château de Barbeyrolles
  83580 Gassin
  tel. : 04.94.56.33.58

Bandol

Château Pradeaux
  83270 Saint-Cyr-sur-Mer
  tel. : 04.94.32.10.21
Château de Pibarnon
  83740 La Cadière
  tel. : 04.94.90.12.73
Château Romassan
  Clos Mireille
  83250 La Londe-les-Maures
  tel. : 04.93.34.38.91
Domaine Tempier
  83330 Plan-du-Castellet
  tel. : 04.94.98.70.21

Cassis

Clos Sainte-Magdeleine
  13260 Cassis
  tel. : 04.42.01.70.28

Coteaux d'Aix and Les Baux-de-Provence

Mas-Sainte-Berthe
  13520 Les Baux-de-Provence
  tel. : 04.90.54.39.01
Domaine de Trévallon
  Avenue Notre Dame
  du Château
  13150 Saint-Etienne-du-Grès
  tel. : 04.90.49.06.00
Château Revelette
  13490 Jouques
  tel. : 04.42.63.75.43
Château Calissanne
  13680 Lançon
  tel. : 04.90.42.63.03

CORBIÈRES AND LANGUEDOC-ROUSSILLON

Château de Lastours
  11490 Portel-des-Corbières
  tel. : 04.68.48.29.17
Château des Estanilles
  34480 Cabrerolles
  tel. : 04.67.90.29.25
Château de Saint-Martin la Garrigue
  34530 Montagnac
  tel. : 04.67.24.00.40
Mas de Daumas Gassac
  34150 Aniane
  tel. : 04.67.57.71.28

DESSERT WINES

Muscat

Cave des Vignerons
de Beaumes-de-Venise
  84190 Beaumes-de-Venise
  tel. : 04.90.12.41.00
Domaine de Durban
  84190 Beaumes-de-Venise
  tel. : 04.90.62.94.26

Maury

Mas Amiel
  66460 Maury
  tel. : 04.68.29.01.02

Rasteau

Domaine de la Soumade
  84110 Rasteau
  tel. : 04.90.46.11.26

Corsican Wine

Clos Nicrosi
  20247 Rogliano
  tel. : 04.95.35.41.17
Antoine Arena
  20253 Patrimonio
  tel. : 04.95.37.08.27

Banyuls

Cellier des Templiers
  66652 Banyuls
  tel. : 04.68.98.36.70
Coopérative de l'Etoile
  66650 Banyuls
  tel. : 04.68.88.00.10
Domaine du Mas Blanc
  66650 Banyuls
  tel. : 04.68.88.32.12

JURA

Vin Jaune et Côtes-du-Jura

Château d'Arlay
  39140 Arlay
  tel. : 03.84.85.04.22
Domaine André-Tissot
  39600 Montigny-lès-Arsures
  tel. : 03.84.66.08.27

Arbois

Frédéric Lornet
  39600 Montigny-lès-Arsures
  tel. : 03.84.37.44.95

If you live far from the hills of Provence, most of the herbs and other ingredients for these recipes can be easily found in any gourmet shop, upscale supermarket, vegetarian or "whole foods" store. No problem if you live in California or a major city. But for those of you who depend on your neighborhood grocery store where "herbes de provence" are limited to rubbery curly-leafed parsley and crushed herbs in a bottle, or if the French wine aisle stops at Bordeaux, why not go online? A few suggested sites:

www.herbs.com
As stressed throughout this book, the freshest herbs are those you pick from your own garden. Herbs.com offers an online catalogue with an amazing selection of both plants and seeds—including most of the herbs cited in this book. If you are not yet on the web, order by fax or phone.
tel: 1.905.640.6677 (Canada)

fax: 1.905.640.6641
Goodwood, Ontario, Canada
LOC 1A0

www.thespicehouse.com
Until you can harvest from your own garden, try visiting the Spice House. While most of herbs on offer are dried, you can find whole juniper berries and needles of rosemary.
The Spice House
tel: (847) 328-3711
fax: (847) 328-3631
1941 Central Street,
Evanston, IL 60201
tel: (414) 272-0977
fax: (414) 272-1271
1031 N. Old World Third Street,
Milwaukee, WI 53203

www.provence-beyond.com
This is a wonderful site for getting to know the back roads of Provence. Includes a good guide to Provençal

herbs and wines. Many of the wineries list e-mail addresses or web sites.

www.globalfoodmarket.com
The herbs are dried but this could be your best bet for finding the French sea salt and regional olive oils called for in our recipes.

www.wine.com
A short, but decent, list of wines from Provence, which can be shipped to most of the United States.

www.primewines.com
A good choice of vintage wines from Provence and great links to other sites. Ships to most of the United States.

www.amisduvin.com
For readers in the UK, this is the site to visit. A very substantial offering of wines from Provence, which can be shipped to the UK.

Acknowledgments

Many of the photographs in this book were taken in the lovely homes and enchanting gardens of Jacques and Martine Machurot, Giorgio and Irène Silvagni, Michel and Nicky Chavaux, and Jacques and Nicole Martin-Raget. I thank them all for their kindness and their hospitality.

Thanks are also due to Clara Limages, Bertrand Colombier, Bruno Dion, John Malkovich, Pierre Hermé, Elisabeth Bourgeois, Edith Mézard, Giorgio and Irène Salvagni, to Lilou, Sandra, and Gaby, to Alain Rubio, Catherine Coste, Mireille Anselme, Mimi Parnel and Mimi Desana, Madame Zaza of Marseilles, Paul and Jeanne Biehn, and Pierre-Grégoire Guinot for having allowed me to pass on their delicious recipes.

Thanks to Nathalie Legier for the recipe for cheeses spiked with herbs.

Thanks also to Jacques Machurot, who with flair and delicacy, provided the perfect wine list to accompany the dishes in this book. Use his suggestions as the basis for an ideal wine cellar.

Finally, thanks to Gilles Martin-Raget for his patience and talent, to Gisou Bavoillot for accompanying me once again on this voyage of discovery, and to Valérie Gautier and Axel Buret, who have done such splendid work on the layout.

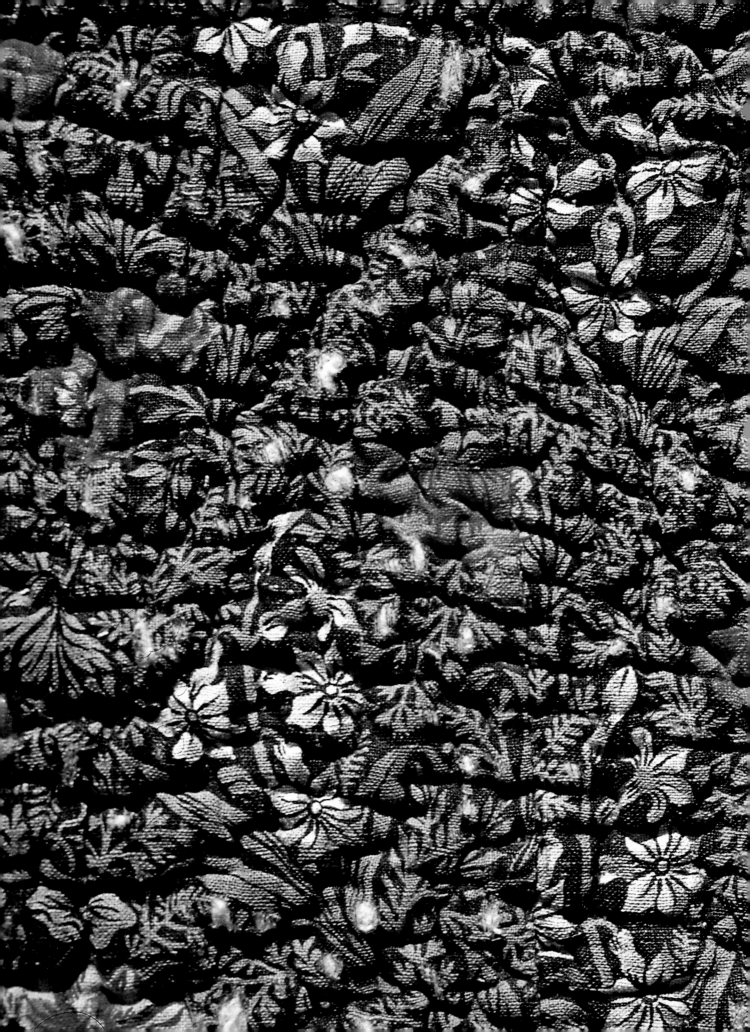